LEADERSHIP
Energy

May your
energy shine!
Cheryl

LEADERSHIP
Energy

Unlocking the Secrets
to Your Success

CHERYL LEITSCHUH, ED.D.

BALBOA
PRESS

A DIVISION OF HAY HOUSE

Balboa Press books may be ordered through booksellers or by contacting:

Balboa Press
A Division of Hay House
1663 Liberty Drive
Bloomington, IN 47403
www.balboapress.com
1-(877) 407-4847

Because of the dynamic nature of the Internet, any web addresses or links contained in this book may have changed since publication and may no longer be valid. The views expressed in this work are solely those of the author and do not necessarily reflect the views of the publisher, and the publisher hereby disclaims any responsibility for them.

The author of this book does not dispense medical advice or prescribe the use of any technique as a form of treatment for physical, emotional, or medical problems without the advice of a physician, either directly or indirectly. The intent of the author is only to offer information of a general nature to help you in your quest for emotional and spiritual well-being. In the event you use any of the information in this book for yourself, which is your constitutional right, the author and the publisher assume no responsibility for your actions.

Any people depicted in stock imagery provided by Thinkstock are models, and such images are being used for illustrative purposes only.
Certain stock imagery © Thinkstock.

Printed in the United States of America.

ISBN: 978-1-4525-7758-6 (sc)
ISBN: 978-1-4525-7760-9 (hc)
ISBN: 978-1-4525-7759-3 (e)

Library of Congress Control Number: 2013912265

Balboa Press rev. date: 07/15/2013

To my husband, Pat, who has always been there no matter what new adventure I choose to undertake!

Contents

Introduction . . . . *ix*

Connection To Self

Chapter 1   iTrust 3
Chapter 2   iConnect 15

Connection To Others

Chapter 3   iAchieve 29
Chapter 4   iCare 41
Chapter 5   iSpeak. 53

Seeing The Big Picture

Chapter 6   iSee 67
Chapter 7   iUnderstand .77

Putting It All Together

Chapter 8   Where To From Here? 89

Appendix Leadership Survey. *95*
Acknowledgements *103*
Resource list *105*

Introduction

» Others think I am an effective leader, but I'm not so sure.

» I lose my confidence as a leader. Am I doing the right thing?

» How do I motivate others to do what I need them to do?

» I love to learn new leadership tools.

If this sounds like you, you've picked the right book. If you are reading this book, you are most likely in a leadership role. You have interest in expanding your leadership effectiveness, and are willing to explore new areas.

This book will help you recognize and change leadership habits that, at the very least don't work or, at worst, cause you to lose sleep. It will go beyond traditional leadership concepts. Through this new knowledge you will gain confidence, create a deeper alignment with yourself, and acquire the best strategies for your own unique style of leadership. The empowerment and clarity of direction you receive will improve and streamline your life and your leadership of others.

The time-tested knowledge based in the eastern understanding of bio-energy will transform your concepts of traditional leadership competency information. You'll have the chance to build awareness that will shift your confidence, strengthen your connection to others, and create clear focus and direction. It will expand your leadership success exponentially by unlocking and connecting a critical area that, until now, has not fit with our western thinking.

Some of you may find the information "New Age" and be resistant to the expansion of the mindset this book provides. It is not my intention to lead you down an uncomfortable or impractical path. Rather, I will share with you real life examples of how this important addition to traditional leadership models will shift your ability to handle those nagging leadership issues that keep you from maximizing your potential.

I have been working as a leadership development coach, trainer, and consultant for more than twenty years. Over the years, I have watched leadership development change and grow in foundational concepts. When I began my practice, the leadership development world had defined leadership traits and competencies. The focus was to train everyone to build strengths in all areas of leadership competencies. Over time, organizations and individuals began to realize that this strategy was not realistic. We each have unique strengths that lend themselves to certain competencies and not to others. Focusing on building all competencies only dilutes the use of our strengths. Our brains can only focus on one or two things at a time. When we focus on building all competencies, we neglect using what comes naturally and easily. We then become mediocre in all competencies. This leads to a frustrated leader! Additionally, this thinking did not lead to effective leadership and improved performance for the organization.

The next phase of leadership development was focus on leadership styles. The foundational idea in this phase was that awareness of style and targeted behavioral changes would lead to more effective leaders. Companies experienced some improvement in results. Individual satisfaction for the leaders and their effectiveness began to increase. We were on the right track!

The most recent change in leadership development has been the focus on strengths and on casting leaders into the roles that best fit their strengths. Great strides were seen in leadership effectiveness, as well as a return in measureable results.

This book will add to the current expansion of knowledge, awareness, effectiveness, and results in the field of leadership. In addition, you will have practical tools you can use at the moment of need.

Several definitions are needed before you move into the content of this book.

First is the definition of leadership. Leadership, as it pertains to this book, is the ability to take your aspirations and inspire others to deliver actionable results. Aspirations are the passion to focus on a future result. Inspiration is the capacity to enroll others to use their aspirations not only for the benefit of an organization, but to satisfy their personal desires and to create measurable outcomes. Actionable results are the key measuring sticks used to determine success.

Bio-energy concepts may be new to many of you. Let me provide a simplified context of bio-energy information to assist as you navigate this book.

Bio-energy is rooted in time tested eastern philosophies. The foundation of this knowledge base is that as effective human beings, we need to be aware of the energy functioning in our bodies. This deck of knowledge has been researched and proven accurate over time.

What does this look like? Our energy templates are influenced by emotional reactions to experiences in our world. These emotional reactions become set in our physical bodies. There are seven primary bio-energy templates in our bodies. The templates become either open or closed depending on the situation, our age and sophistication of life development, and the emotions we experience. If the bio-energy template is open, we create effective connections with others and ourselves. We solve problems and are able to use our gifts to achieve our goals, both personally and professionally. If the bio-energy template is closed, we experience discomfort, both physically and emotionally. This leads to ineffective connections with others and ourselves. We struggle to solve problems and this limits our ability to achieve our goals.

The bio-energy disciplines expand from awareness to established daily practices. They provide an avenue of practical, pro-active problem solving through the awareness and alignment of your energy systems. In eastern cultures, children are taught how to access this information at a very young age through practicing disciplines included in their daily school schedule. Practices such as yoga and meditation are examples of practices related to bio-energy.

This book is not about teaching you yoga and meditation. It is about assisting you in accessing this time-tested knowledge and allowing you to expand beyond the limits of our western thinking. Think about how you were taught in school. Most of us were taught from a young age to learn by thinking or reading. Emotional and/or physical awareness were not a component of learning. Instead physical and emotional awareness were segmented into separate compartments. Do you want to increase your physical strength? Go to the gym. Do you have emotional distress? See a therapist. However, if you wanted to include emotional and physical awareness to assist in solving problems, or look at the possible solutions from this broader perspective, impossible! Yet, the truth is, it is through having emotional and physical awareness that we can best learn, access, and provide pro-active and effective solutions.

Let me give you an example. You are asked to deliver an important presentation to your company's senior leadership team. You have done presentations before but never to this level in the organization. The presentation is one hour away. What are you feeling in your body and where?

Typically, when I ask this question, I hear, "I'm excited" or "I'm nervous" or "I feel like I want to throw up." These are statements of thought and emotion. They usually lead to a level of awareness, but typically we are not taught to use them to create solutions. Instead, when we experience this awareness, we usually shut it down.

What happens in your body when you are nervous? What are the clues to feeling nervous or excited? It might be that your stomach feels queasy. Perhaps you can't stop moving around. Or, maybe, your hands are clenched. What is it for you?

In bio-energy strategies, you would recognize the specific body reaction and you would focus on releasing and expanding the energy in that area of your body. For example, if you were aware that your hands are clenched, you would focus on your hands and actively release and stretch your hands. Now you are honoring your bio-energy system and using it to create a solution, rather than block or ignore its message.

Think of this process like a river. Picture the flow of water on a calm day. Watch as the water flows easily and gently down the river. Now look down the river. You will find a place where rocks change the flow of the water. Does the water keep moving? Yes, but not without turbulence. The size and the number of the rocks impact the size and the amount of the turbulence. Where the rocks come from does not matter; the fact that they exist is what creates the impact.

Flowing water is what we strive for in an open bio-energy system. The rocks are like the emotions that build because of life situations and your own level of development. If we learn to recognize the emotions early, then we can make the decisions necessary to keep the river flowing. If we allow the rocks to build, then we create greater turbulence.

Now imagine that an ambitious beaver has built a dam across the river. The water is backing up behind the dam. Downstream from the dam, the water is significantly shallow with little to no water flow. How long will the unbalanced water flow continue? It depends on how long the dam can take the pressure from the blocked water flow. It may last a long time or a short time. When it can no longer take the pressure, the dam will break and the water flow will be uncertain. Perhaps it will be slow and trickling, or it could cause floods. If we are aware of the dam, we can control its opening and, thus, the flow of the water.

For some, the emotional impact of certain situations can create problems. Or being too young and unable to articulate or understand the emotional impact will create blocked energies, just like the dam blocks the water in the river. Awareness makes it possible to carefully and intentionally control the opening of these emotions and restore the flow of our energy.

Energy is similar to the river. If we keep the river of energy calm and clear, it flows peacefully and effectively. If we allow "rocks" to gather, there will be turbulence. The size and amount of the turbulence will depend on the size of the energy blocks. Or we can close down the energy flow by allowing our energies to become blocked. Awareness of our biological signals that tell us our energy is blocked is the key to determining what outcomes we want and what strategies we'll use to get there.

Contrast this with cognitive strategies such as "tell yourself to relax' or "picture yourself successfully delivering the presentation". My experience with hundreds of clients who have tried this method usually produces one of two results.

» Your brain fights the thoughts and your physical signals can turn into symptoms that increase in severity.

» It eventually does calm your anxiety.

So, if cognitive strategies sometimes work, then what's the problem? There is a chance that they won't work and then your symptoms will increase. Or, waiting for it to work may be too time consuming. If you have minutes to go before your presentation, you need a new model that will work now.

The old model taught you to be an observer of your thoughts. These thoughts generated behaviors, which influenced results. In **The Leadership Energy Model**, in addition to your thoughts, you will become aware of your emotional and physical energy signals triggered by a given situation. Broadening the scope of your awareness will give you access to more choiceful behavior and, in turn, lead to more satisfying results. Using this model not only creates a stronger awareness, but it gives you additional tools to bring about more effective solutions.

The Leadership Energy Model will focus on how to use these bio-energy strategies to address your leadership needs. Our current models of leadership include leadership competencies, skills, and traits. These fall into the thought and behavior categories of awareness. In this model, I add the seven categories of bio-energy study and their impact on leadership. The leadership competencies, skills and traits are not to be ignored. By adding the bio-energy component, you will open, expand, and integrate this energy with thoughts and behaviors for more effective results. By keeping the energy flow similar to the flow of a calm river, your life and your leadership will be empowered to move in the direction you desire.

The format of this book is designed to expand your learning in each of the energy dimensions. Throughout this book you will follow two leaders, Stephanie and Daniel, as they experience common leadership issues. Each chapter begins with the story of a leadership dilemma encountered by one of the leaders. After the initial story, you will learn more about the leadership competencies and the bio-energy components related to each chapter's focus. My intent here is to increase your understanding of bio-energy through awareness of emotional and physical signals and symptoms. I will share additional stories to help you apply what you are learning.

The final tool is focused action-learning assignments to help you continue to open and expand your energy system. Action learning is a technique that goes beyond merely reading information. It asks you to apply the learning while observing the results you experience. It is an effective way to bring the concepts in this book to real life applications.

Each chapter concludes with a story of how Stephanie or Daniel's new understanding and awareness of the bio-energy information helped them make different decisions that created changes in their thoughts and behavior, and, in the end, generated different, more satisfying outcomes. Subtle internal changes, happening within a fraction of a second and not noticeable to the outside world, can change everything. This book will help you understand, isolate, and reproduce such changes.

The book wraps up with a chapter focused on putting it all together called "Where To From Here?" This summary chapter reflects on what an effective leader does and how they impact others. It will also consider implications for your future. I have also included a list of additional resources.

Now it is time to open the bio-energy river of knowledge. I hope you enjoy the journey and take from this book the awareness, knowledge, and tools that will expand your leadership confidence, focus, and success. Let the journey begin...

PART ONE

Connection To Self

The book format is divided into three sections. Part one's focus is Connection to Self. Part two addresses Connection to Others. Part three expands to Seeing the Big Picture.

Part One is about YOU! This might be the most important part of the book, because if you don't get this right, nothing else works.

Chapter One: iTrust
"I am successful because I am here."

Chapter Two: iConnect
"I want to connect and share myself with others."

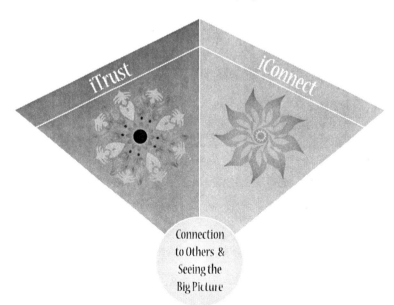

CHAPTER ONE

iTrust

"I am successful because I am here."

MEET STEPHANIE. STEPHANIE is a talented professional who has been in her career 15 years. Her career has encompassed several leadership positions, but she is continually passed over for the next "big" step in her career. From the outside, she is competent, achieves what is asked of her, and is respected among senior leadership as well as her peers. Internally, she worries that she will not meet the expectations of others. She wants to advance, but is frustrated that no one selects her for the next position. She questions what she needs to do to move forward.

Stephanie exhibits leadership skills. These include effective communication, managing her time, and creating positive accountability. Yet, she worries and lacks confidence in what she does. Until she deals with her worry and self-doubt, her leadership skills will not be enough to advance her career. The potential joy she would have in achieving her goals will be lost.

Let's join Stephanie as she faces one of her leadership scenarios....

Stephanie's meeting with her boss, Steve, is at 11:00 A.M. He had requested the meeting with no indication of an agenda. She wants to

3

be early so she leaves her office, makes the short trip to his office, and nervously waits outside his door.

Steve greets her as he notices her waiting, "Hi, Steph! Come on in."

Stephanie enters his office, holding her notepad tightly to her chest. She sits at the table and puts her blank notepad on the table. He asks if she would like coffee and she says "no." *Had she done something wrong?* She worries. *Why does he want to meet with me? I must have done something wrong on the Holcolm project, but after last night's lost sleep over worrying what it could be, I still have no idea.*

Steve begins, "Steph, you have done such an incredible job on the Holcolm project. We've decided to pull you from that project and assign you to our newest project, the City of Albany."

Steph replies, "Oh, I really didn't do anything special on the Holcolm project. It was my team who really delivered. The City of Albany is such a new effort. I've never done anything like that before. Are you sure I'm ready?"

Steve quickly responds, "Stephanie, this is a huge opportunity for you. I really want you on this project. No matter what you say, we know you were the driving force on the Holcolm project. You have things so organized that we are confident we can turn things over to Tom. Can I count you in on Albany?"

"I...I...I...suppose..." Stephanie stammers as she tries to understand what is being offered. Her thoughts spin. *Can I do it? Will this be the project that is too much for me? How will I know if this is the right move?*

"Great!" replies Steve. "Our first meeting will be next Monday at 2:00. See you there."

Stephanie picks up her empty notepad and leaves the office. As she walks back to her desk, she continues to worry. *Am I ready for this? I've wanted to move forward in my career and now is the chance but...am I really ready?*

Stephanie's story describes a common theme among leaders desiring new opportunities while, at the same time, questioning their ability to succeed. Where does this questioning come from and more importantly, how does she shift to stepping up with greater confidence?

The Leadership Competencies

Let's start with leadership competencies. Competencies are expected behaviors displayed by a leader. There are sixty-seven competencies as defined by Lominger Institutes Career Architect. The two most relevant to iTrust energy are Self-Knowledge and Action Oriented. Let's look at each competency and the impact on leadership behaviors from two perspectives: open iTrust energy and closed iTrust energy.

The leader with open iTrust energy will be skilled in the area of Self-Knowledge. They know their personal strengths, opportunities, and limitations. They seek feedback and gain insights from mistakes. They look forward to balanced performance reviews and career discussions addressing both the positive and negative aspects. The leader with closed iTrust energy may be too self-critical. They do not know themselves well and are hesitant to receive feedback, whether positive or negative. They may often avoid conversations about their career, assuming it will be negative in nature.

The Action Oriented competency is observed in the open iTrust leader as someone who enjoys his or her work. They are full of energy and willing to be challenged. They do not fear taking action, even with a minimum of planning or information. The closed iTrust energy impacts action orientation through a hesitancy to act or in resisting challenging goals. Others may see leaders with closed iTrust energy as lacking confidence and unwilling to take risks.

While the leadership competencies seem fairly straightforward, the underlying energy dynamic carries the secrets to your effectiveness. Let's talk further about the energy ingredient.

The Energy Ingredient

The iTrust statement is "I am successful because I am here." The implication of this statement is that we are able to trust our ability to find solutions. In the bio-energy world this comes from a belief in ourselves. Fear is the block that inhibits the energy river from flowing. Fear is like a dam built by a beaver. Energy does not flow if we are fearful. If we believe we need to perform to be successful or that we are not capable to solve the problems we face, we lack trust in ourselves. This translates into lack of trust in others. How can we possibly believe that others see us as successful when we secretly believe we are not? To others, our reactions portray a lack of confidence. And it's true! If we are questioning ourselves, lack of confidence ensues.

But isn't questioning good? Problem solving thoughts and questions are positive. Fear based thoughts and questions create blocks. If you are faced with a new situation that requires you to stretch your skills and acquire new information, do you determine the steps you will need to assist you? Or, do you question your ability to take on this new situation? If your thoughts are, "I need to generate a list of what I can do and whom I will need for additional information," you are in a healthy, problem-solving state of trusting yourself. If you are saying to yourself, "I'm sure this will be the time I will fail," you are in a fear-based block of iTrust energy.

We all experience both types of internal questioning. The key is awareness. Thoughts can be the most common level of awareness. The secret to unlocking the iTrust energy lies in the emotional and physical development of this energy.

How does iTrust energy develop? Even before you were born, you were forming an emotional understanding of how the world works. These understandings become emotional templates stored in your body. In other words, the experiences you have from pre-birth to six months old become a base of emotional perceptions about the world. In contrast, psychology would say that your thoughts are the perceptions that guide your life. If you don't like what is happening, change your thoughts.

That makes sense unless you consider that the iTrust element is developed in the pre-birth to six-month time frame. Clearly, language skills are not yet developed, so you cannot put labels or thoughts on your experience. At this point in your life, you only have emotions. These emotional templates set the stage for your later thought development.

For example, if you are an infant who experiences the world as non-responsive to your cries, you become fearful of not being heard. This becomes the emotional template that is stored in your body. As you grow and begin to develop language skills, you hesitate to trust others and you label these new experiences based on your past emotional template. So, you may say, "People just aren't there for me." The thoughts may also include, "I must not be worthy for others to be there for me." The early blocks to the iTrust energy become the basis for your current and future thought structure.

Conversely, if you are an infant who experiences the world as responsive to your cries, the emotional energy template is set to be willing to believe that others see you as valuable just because you were born. The emotional and physical blocks to iTrust energy would not exist. You would approach new situations with curiosity and the willingness to try new things.

So how do we, as leaders, use this information? We must start by paying attention to our physical and emotional responses. Stephanie's emotions of nervousness and uncertainty about her own capabilities are classic symptoms that the iTrust energy has been blocked. Think of this like the rock in the river. The "rock" or "block" forms turbulence in the water. If the rock is small, the turbulence is small. If the rock is large, so is the turbulence. How was the block formed? This may stem from issues early in her life. Early life issues can include abuse, neglect or expectations from performance-based conditional love. In either case, the message is "You are not worthy to be here unless you prove it." Stephanie's lack of confidence will always be present, no matter what the outside world tells her.

Some would consider this a counseling or therapy issue, depending on its severity. However, talking alone, which is often the case in therapy, will not move this block. Remember, this is a block formed in the pre-language period from pre-birth to six-months. Therapy may help, but only if it includes understanding the emotional and physical dynamics of the problem.

Individuals with a pattern of closed iTrust energy show both emotional and physical patterns. If the iTrust energy is open, you feel like you belong and have strong connections with family, friends, and co-workers. If the iTrust energy is closed, you carry an underlying sense of not belonging or being worthy.

Eastern philosophies recognize that the energy templates are stored in our body. They identify physical symptoms that may indicate challenges when energy is closed. The physical symptoms of closed iTrust energy may include eating disorders, problems with feet or legs, spinal problems or immune-related disorders. In western cultures, there is separation of these symptoms as "health issues" with little connection to the blocks that affect our lives, relationships, career, and leadership. Awareness of all aspects of yourself is a critical ingredient to unlock the secrets to your success.

So what can you do to immediately address these iTrust bio-energy symptoms? People tend to close or block the iTrust energies when they are frightened. To open the energies, they must recognize the fear *at that moment* and then calm the symptoms. Ignoring them only creates more symptoms. If the lower back hurts, take time to stretch and move. Your goal is to assure the body that you hear its message and are there to take care of it. Many of my clients say to me, "I just need to ignore it until a later time." What happens when a six-month-old infant cries and you don't respond? Don't they scream louder? By ignoring the physical message, you only strengthen the blocked energy.

What symptoms do you ignore? What would happen if you addressed them as close to the moment as you could? What could you do? How would it help?

Awareness Activities

If the iTrust energy has been blocked for a long time and you have unintentionally cemented the block in your body, there are additional activities that will assist in gently opening and expanding the iTrust energy. Let me share with you activities that have worked with my clients.

Creating Awareness of Your Unique Strengths

We need a sense of why we are here and what makes us unique. Our current world of work asks us to give up our unique expressions of self to do what is best for the organization. From an organization perspective, we create employees that become apathetic and lethargic. Lack of confidence, an unclear focus and uncertain personal purpose can dominate an individual's perspective.

The activities associated with identifying your unique strengths include assessments or self-reflection exercises. One exercise is to create a timeline of all the jobs you have had throughout your lifetime. This includes the lemonade stand you had at five years old or the lawn-moving job you had at ten years old. Identify what you enjoyed in each job and what you didn't enjoy. As you complete the exercise, notice the patterns that occur. Your unique strengths will show a pattern, even at a very early age. This is your opportunity to step back and observe what the unique pattern is for you!

Let me tell you about Tom. Tom was much like Stephanie. He was constantly fearful and worried over not delivering what others expected. He was mistrustful of others. "They must want more than that." "They say they like my work but what do they really think?"

Tom is typical of many successful high-achievers whose iTrust energy has been impacted, either early in life, or over time in his adult life. As this pattern progresses, high achievers live out an unhealthy level of over-achieving or people pleasing. This causes them to try to be everything to everyone, ignoring their own needs. Tom's expectations for himself also impacted his team. They were confused, uncertain, and could not meet Tom's expectations.

Bosses, peers and employees saw Tom as incredibly competent, but he lacked a work-life balance. He believed he would be free of the fear and the worry of not being enough if he worked harder. Additionally, Tom suffered from adrenal insufficiency. Symptoms included chronic fatigue, weight loss and headaches. His doctor kept telling him that he needed to slow down, but Tom believed that if he took enough medication, he could control this "silly physical issue".

It took a hospitalization for Tom to realize he couldn't out-work his physical and emotional blocks. After leaving the hospital, he finally decided to take things seriously. He was skeptical that coaching would help, but he was willing to give it a try.

A two-fold focus was necessary. First, Tom clarified his unique strengths through a series of assessments and self-reflection exercises. How did this help? Tom, like others with closed iTrust energy, often miss others recognizing and applauding their unique strengths. Through completing these exercises, Tom's understanding of who he is and what he does to create success puts him on a more level playing field with high iTrust energy leaders. Expanding the awareness and pride of a person's unique qualities leads to expanded iTrust energy.

Second, Tom learned to stay grounded in the present moment. He needs to listen to himself, while providing practical solutions to things he can immediately address. His assignment was to stop twice a day and answer two questions. "What am I feeling *right now*? What can I do to calm or appreciate this feeling *right now*?"

Over the course of three months, Tom's physical symptoms decreased, he reported feeling a sense of relief from fear and worry, and his team reported a greater sense of accomplishment. Is Tom done? No! He will always need to pay attention to this pattern of self-doubt, worry, and the lack of trust in himself. However, he now has tools to use in the short-term and long-term.

Identifying Your Purpose in Life

ITrust energy increases every time you take an action that aligns with your purpose. Dr. Beatrice Berry, author of *I'm On My Way But Your Foot Is On My Head*, states, "When you walk with purpose, you collide with destiny." What is your purpose? Why do you get out of bed every morning? Define what you want this life to be. Every day is a clean slate and an opportunity to do one thing to honor and live your purpose. You can only do this if you are free of fear and grounded in today. It is like sewing a quilt. A beautiful quilt takes time and patience. We need to cut each block, sew each seam and with time, it becomes a work of art. Patience is often the struggle of high achievers. By recognizing each day as your "quilt work", you stay grounded in the present, trust your unique contributions, and create the purpose driven success you desire and deserve.

Other Suggestions

If you struggle with keeping the iTrust energy open, there are several additional activities that will support you. These activities are designed to keep you focused in the present and appreciate what is happening right now. These activities are key to your effectiveness as a leader. Take a look at the list.

> » Jogging
> » Foot massage
> » Pounding your feet on the floor several times a day
> » Walk barefoot outside in the grass or sand
> » Move!
> » Sit with your back against a tree
> » Eat
> » Play with children
> » Do some gardening

Are you surprised by the list? Don't over-analyze these suggestions by asking, "How do they do that?" The suggestions come from heavily researched bio-energy tools. The suggested activities target grounding yourself and focusing on the present moment. These are key ingredients to utilizing the iTrust energy.

Action Learning

This action learning exercise focuses on the iTrust energy. As you work on the iTrust energy, it is important to recognize the physical aspect of your body that houses this energy. For the iTrust energy, this is located at the base of your spine. The emotional energy that either opens, becomes blocked, or closes is centered in this area.

Before you begin, focus your awareness on the base of your spine. Suggestions to add focus include: holding your hand over this area, looking in the mirror specifically observing this area, or using a word or two to describe the feelings in this area before you begin. It may feel strange to focus on your body to solve leadership and trust issues, but challenge yourself!

Here is an exercise to increase your awareness and begin the shift:

1. What is one area in which you currently feel fear or worry? What physical symptoms do you recognize that let you know you are fearful or anxious? If you are not used to connecting emotional responses to physical symptoms, this may seem uncomfortable at first. If you only identify one symptom, that is progress! The more often you do this exercise, the more awareness you will create.

2. On a scale of 1-10 (1-low; 10-high) how strong is the fear or worry?

3. What would it look like if you improved the score by 2 points? Not perfect—just 2 points. Focus on the physical sensations you would be experiencing. Remember, iTrust is a physical template created by an emotional experience. Where would you feel it differently in your body? How would you notice the difference?

4. The following is a list of activities that assist in shifting from closed iTrust energy to open iTrust energy. Choose one of these activities.

   » Jogging
   » Foot massage
   » Pounding your feet on the floor several times a day
   » Walk barefoot outside in the grass or sand
   » Move!
   » Sit with your back against a tree
   » Eat
   » Play with children

» Do some gardening

5. Implement the activity you have chosen for just one day.

6. At the end of the day, answer these questions:

   » Has your worry or fear score changed today?

   » Will you use the technique you chose again tomorrow?

   » If yes, continue tomorrow and answer these same questions at the end of the day.

   » If no, choose another suggested technique. Try it for one day and answer these questions again.

Stephanie revisited

It is 1:00 PM on Monday and the first meeting for the Albany project is scheduled for 2:00 PM. Stephanie could feel the nervousness building. She had trouble swallowing. Her hands were clammy and her stomach was fluttering. She had a desk full of work and items to take care of for the Holcolm project. Another hour of work on Holcolm would be great, BUT would it help her address her nervousness?

Stephanie had not gone to lunch yet. She knows she needs to calm the nervousness before that meeting. She decides to wander outside to a small park next to her office. Yes, the Holcolm project needed more work, but her nervousness needed to take priority.

She sits down on a bench and slowly eats her lunch. She sees children playing on the swings. Her thoughts begin to take over as she analyzes every possible scenario for the upcoming meeting. She tells herself *Stop this Stephanie! This will not help! Focus on the children playing, feel the ground beneath your feet, enjoy the warmth of the sun and slowly eat your lunch.* As she finishes, she is still wondering what will happen at the 2:00 meeting. She feels calmer; less nervous but still wondering.

She walks back to her office. It is 1:50 PM. She picks up her notepad and walks to the conference room for the meeting.

The next two hours are filled with new data about the Albany project. Flipcharts are posted throughout the room as project needs are identified and tasks assigned. As the list grows, Stephanie begins to see where she and her team can be a great resource for this project. At times during the meeting, she feels her nervousness and her doubts increase. She takes a breath, feels the floor beneath her feet, and actively works to stay curious and open versus fearful and nervous.

As the tasks and roles are assigned, Stephanie volunteers for several tasks that fit well with the team's strengths. She also agrees to a few that will be a stretch, knowing she will figure it out later.

As she prepares to leave the meeting, Steve asks if she has a minute to talk. Everyone leaves the room. Steve comments, "Steph, I wasn't sure what to expect from you at today's meeting because you were so unsure when we met last week. I am delighted that you identified where you fit and that you have taken on this new assignment!"

As Stephanie walks back to her office, she has a smile on her face. She is delighted with herself. Will she face fear and uncertainty again? Most likely. It has always been a pattern for her. But today, she was able to choose tools to help her stay calm, focused and effective.

CHAPTER TWO

iConnect

"I want to connect and share myself with others."

MEET DANIEL. DANIEL has a very strong desire to advance in his career to the Division Director's position. He works tirelessly, sometimes seventy to eighty hours per week, and achieves great results. Although he has a team that reports to him, he complains that he has no one to whom he can delegate work. During his performance reviews, he consistently hears that he needs to engage and develop his team. He thinks he is helping to develop other people's potential, but he is not able to connect in a way that brings out the best in his team. He assumes it is the company's fault that they have hired people who can't live up to his expectations.

Daniel demonstrates positive leadership traits. He is passionate, self-directed, and focused. While he knows he needs to develop and engage others, he struggles with understanding why what he is doing is not working for him. Until he understands what is blocking this energy to connect, he will also lack the effectiveness to advance his career.

Let's follow Daniel as he faces a challenge in his leadership effectiveness.........

Daniel sits in his office, door closed, and thinks about the last three months. Three months ago today, he was promoted to Department Manager. What a great day that was! He had been working toward that position for years. Finally he had arrived! Arrived where, he wonders. Today has been one of the worst days of his entire career.

Daniel's thoughts move to the conversation he had just completed with Julie, the Director of Human Resources. Four of his staff had resigned in the last three weeks. His meeting with Julie was to review the exit interviews she had conducted to learn more about why they had left. The list included:

» Daniel's expectations are too high.

» He doesn't give anyone credit for the work they did—he just piles on more work.

» Because he works seventy to eighty hours per week, it doesn't mean everyone else wants to do the same.

» All fun in the department is gone.

They wanted fun! And my expectations were too high! Don't they know what it takes to get ahead in this organization? Daniel's anger increases as he continues to think about the feedback. *Don't they value how hard I work for them and the organization? They are so wrong! Good riddance!*

Daniel takes a deep breath, shakes his head, and turns the attention to his desk. It's five o'clock. He has a list of things to complete before he goes home. He says out loud, "Enough of that. I need to get back to what is important."

Daniel's story is typical of a leader struggling with the closed iConnect energy.

The Leadership Competencies

There are three key leadership competencies that are relevant to iConnect energy: Interpersonal Savvy, the Ability to Delegate, and Work/Life Balance. Let me explain what the leadership behavior looks like when the energy is open versus when the energy is closed.

Interpersonal Savvy is a key competency for effective leadership. We know that the biggest reason people leave organizations is their relationship with their immediate supervisor. When the iConnect energy is open, leaders enjoy all kinds of people and take time to relate to them. They build appropriate rapport along with constructive and effective relationships. When iConnect energy is closed, one of two behaviors occurs.

> » The leader spends too much time building a network among people, but may not be a credible take-charge leader.

> » The leader has a difficult time building relationships. Others see the leader as lacking approachability. This leader may be excessively work oriented and intense. He/she may be seen as judgmental or arrogant. The leader is often critical and attacks others versus providing effective feedback and dialogue.

These behaviors block the desire for others to connect with the leader.

Delegation is another key competency that creates effective leadership and relationship development. Open iConnect energy is found in leaders who clearly and comfortably delegate mundane tasks, as well as important tasks and decisions. They trust others to perform and let direct reports finish their own work. The employees share in both the responsibility and accountability of tasks.

Closed iConnect energy affects delegation behaviors in one of two ways.

> » Leaders who over-delegate without providing guidance or help. They have unrealistic expectations, which, in turn, become self-fulfilling prophecies, as the individual cannot deliver the results the leader expects.

> » Leaders who do not believe in or trust delegation. They don't know how to empower others, so they either do it themselves, or, if they do delegate, they are constantly micro managing.

The final competency is Work/Life Balance. The open iConnect leader makes a conscious choice to balance their work and their personal life. This does not necessarily mean equal amounts of time spent on each. What it does mean is that the individual is clear about their personal and professional desires. They actively find pleasure in the whole of their life. Closed iConnect leaders lack balance and pleasure in their life choices. They get bored or cannot relax when not at their job. They may try to force their lack of balance on others and not appreciate their need for finding pleasure in both their work and non-work worlds.

The Energy Ingredient

The leadership competency discussion focuses on behavior. Now let's focus on the energy template that effects this behavior.

The iConnect energy shares the Part One category of Connection To Self with iTrust energy. While iTrust relates to confidence and is impacted by fear, iConnect relates to the desire to connect with others and is impacted by guilt.

iConnect energy is formed between one and three years of age, another pre-language or primitive language period. Just as with iTrust, iConnect energy templates are formed in the body and are created by emotional experiences. Open iConnect energy provides a sense of well-being and pleasure through self-nurturing and self-care. How much we enjoy life and how effectively we connect with others are influenced by this energy. If we are able to experience the joy of self-nurturing and nurturing from others, iConnect energy is open; we enjoy connecting with others and feel valued and respected for who we are. Emotions consistent with open iConnect energy are joy and pleasure.

If we experience guilt for wanting pleasure, our energy tends to become blocked or guarded. When our energy template closes, we work hard to prove to others that we are worthy, valued, and deserving of respect. Emotions consistent with closed iConnect are guilt and anger. Instead of "I want to connect and share myself with others," the energy message is, "I need to protect myself and do things alone."

Let me tell you about Deborah. She is much like Daniel. She works seventy hours a week on a regular basis. Everything is a crisis for her. She constantly wonders, *is my boss happy with what I am doing?* The pressure is enormous, but self created.

Deborah's previous boss had suggested to her that she change this pattern. She was not aware that his goal was to promote her to his position following an upcoming re-organization, which would move him to another position. One of his concerns was her ability to develop someone to replace her. The second concern was that she was over extending herself. Her work ethic went beyond reasonable expectations and was not healthy for her. His goals were clear: develop her replacement and establish better work/life balance.

Deborah was open to coaching and admitted that she felt the pressure to perform. If she didn't, what value did she have? She had dreams of taking vacations in Europe or spending time at a spa. But how could she take vacations? There was always another crisis to solve and she believed that no one could handle things as well as she could. She had also put on forty pounds since taking this position four years ago. Food had become her only source of pleasure.

As Deborah talked about the pressures of her position, she quickly became angry and then felt guilty. She talked about her boss taking advantage of her willingness to step in. She described her team as unwilling to step up to the plate and get things done. Yet, when she talked about a specific event that could have been handled differently, she smiled as she described the number of hours she worked and how she delivered the solution to her boss at midnight on a Saturday. She certainly received positive satisfaction in continuing to be the only one to deliver such results!

Changing iConnect patterns can be challenging. This is a pattern that creates positive reinforcement, particularly in our western culture. Proving our value by getting results is valued and measured by the hours worked. We often hear about the person who went the extra mile to get the job done, versus the person who did a great job of taking care of themselves and others.

So what happened with Deborah? Her boss was moved to a new position and she was not promoted. Despite the encouragement and support, Deborah could not make the changes he requested. When the new boss came in, Deborah thought, "Oh good! A clean slate!" It did begin that way. Her new boss appreciated her willingness to be available and her quick response to solving problems. But, within three months, the new boss quickly became aware of Deborah's unhealthy patterns and started to make the same requests of Deborah. "Develop others to take on tasks." "You don't need to work 24/7, find others to assist you." But the pattern continued.

How does iConnect energy become blocked? The same emotional experiences that can affect iTrust energy also impact iConnect energy. The blocks can occur from abuse, neglect, or trauma. Or they can occur from others who love you only conditionally. At an early age, if you experienced other people in your life enjoying their connection with you and you enjoying your connection with them, iConnect energy will be open and develop naturally.

Awareness Activities

Now let's look at how to change the iConnect energy. You shift the energy from closed to open by learning self-care and self-nurturing. You need to give yourself permission to care for yourself, consistently maintain your well-being and enjoy things that give you pleasure. When you do this for yourself, you respect the need others have to do the same. Similar to iTrust, you can't understand and offer self-care to others if you don't practice it yourself.

In Christy Tryhus's book, *Live Life Beyond The Laundry*, she states, "Many…believe that "Me" Time is selfish…If you do not take "Me" Time, you are likely to feel overwhelmed, stressed, and burned out, or even depressed." She identifies seven steps to the *Creating "Me" Time Tool*. Here are the seven steps.

1. Write down **what do you like to do?** This will create a "Me" Time menu.

2. Ask yourself **why am I not taking time for myself?** This is a critical step. By identifying your challenges and obstacles,

you will be more successful in implementing the "Me" Time strategy.

3. For **seven days,** take **ten minutes** of "Me"Time each day.

4. After the first seven days, **write down how taking time for you made you feel.** Even if there were negative feelings of stress or guilt, write it down, but don't stop taking "Me" Time.

5. **Step it up a notch** by increasing the amount of "Me" Time. For 23 more days, take a minimum of 20 minutes per day.

6. **Journal how you feel** as you continue the commitment to "Me" Time.

7. **Celebrate your success!** Write down how you will celebrate your success as you remain committed and consistent with "Me" Time.

Other Suggestions

There are several activities that support iConnect energy. The basis of these activities is experiencing enjoyment and pleasure. They include:

» Long, warm showers or baths

» Working on creative projects

» Bike riding along the river

» Afternoon naps

» Swimming

» Massages

You may wonder why these activities are individually focused and not about actively connecting with others. The shift can only occur if you value and connect with yourself.

Action Learning

This action learning exercise focuses on the iConnect energy. As you work with the iConnect energy, it is important to remember that it is housed in your body and is located behind your navel. The emotional energy that either opens, becomes blocked, or closes, is centered in this area.

Before you begin, focus your awareness on this area behind your navel. If you want to pinpoint the physical location of iConnect energy even more, you can hold your hand over this area, look in the mirror specifically observing this area, or use a word or two to describe the feelings in this area before you begin.

There are two parts to this exercise. Part one is connecting with and valuing you. Part two is increasing your connection to others.

Part One: Connection to self

1. From the list of supporting activities identified in this chapter, choose one you can incorporate in your daily life. Here is the list.

   » Long, warm showers or baths

   » Working on creative projects

   » Bike riding along the river

   » Afternoon naps

   » Swimming

   » Massages

2. Include this activity in your daily life for thirty days and observe the impact on you and your body. For example, an easy choice may be a long, warm shower or bath each day. What most people typically do is to take a daily shower with little focus on the experience of the shower. You probably focus on planning your day or solving an issue while taking that bath or shower. For the thirty-day period, remove all other thoughts, and focus on the feeling of the warm shower. Nurture and care for yourself as you shower.

3. Journal your reactions each day. It may be only a sentence of two.

That's fine. Just write your reactions. Note: the reactions might be negative, as well as positive. No judgment. Simply complete the activity and journal your reactions for thirty days.

4. After thirty days review your journal and decide if this is an activity you wish to continue. If so, carry on! If not, choose another activity and repeat the exercise again for thirty days. Continue until you find the activities that provide you simple joy and pleasure.

Part Two: Connection to others

1. Identify a relationship in your life. Start with a co-worker or friend.

2. Ask the following questions:

   » Do I feel valued by this person? Why or why not?

   » Do we support and encourage each other or is one of us doing more nurturing? Why or why not?

   » What does this say about me in this relationship?

3. Based on your answers to question 2, identify what you would continue doing in this relationship, what you would stop doing, and what you would start doing.

4. Focus on these changes for one month.

5. Journal your reactions throughout the month.

6. At the end of the month, ask the following questions again:

   » Do I feel valued by this person? Why or why not?

   » Do we support and encourage each other or is one of us doing more nurturing? Why or why not?

   » What does this say about me in this relationship?

7. Decide what you will do differently as you move forward with this relationship.

8. Choose another relationship to focus on for the next month.

Daniel revisited

Three days have passed since the conversation with Julie. Although Daniel didn't like what he heard, he is calmer today. He knows he needs to hear the feedback as an opportunity to grow in his leadership effectiveness. Over the past few days, he realized how fun is missing in his own life. He isn't sure when work took over and fun was sacrificed.

Daniel is ready to make the changes needed to become the leader he knows he can be. His first step is to call a meeting with Ben.

Ben is a hard worker and always gets things done. Daniel knows Ben will be honest with him. He and Ben have enjoyed a great working relationship in the past, before he took on this new position. Perhaps there is an opportunity to rebuild the relationship they once had.

Ben arrived at the office at 9:00 AM. Daniel begins, "Thanks for coming Ben. As you know, we have had four people resign in the last three weeks. I heard from Julie that they left because of my style of management. I want to talk with you and a few others to see if that is true. Would you be open to telling me your thoughts?"

Ben says, "I'll try but…."

"I know. I would also be suspicious of my intentions," replies Daniel. "Just give me as much feedback as you're comfortable sharing. Okay?"

"Okay." replies Ben.

Daniel begins. "One of the comments from a former employee is that we have lost all the fun around here since I took over. Any thoughts on that one?"

Ben laughs. "All work and no fun make Ben a dull boy!"

Daniel laughs, too. He wants to say more but knows he needs to listen, so he remains quiet hoping Ben will go on.

Ben continues, "When Nick was here, we would joke around, take breaks to kick back, and talk about things besides work. You have a way of giving us a look whenever we tell a joke or take a break."

"Can you give me an example?" asks Daniel.

Ben continues, "Sure. Just last week we were sitting in the coffee area. Jill was telling a crazy story about her dog. We were all laughing. You came out of your office, grabbed a cup of coffee, gave us one of your looks, and went back to your office. You didn't join in or say anything, you only gave us a dirty look. We all knew we needed to get back to work immediately."

Daniel has no idea what Ben is talking about. *What day was that,* he wonders. *I must have been thinking about the Murphy project. Last week everything had exploded on that one.*

Daniel responds, "Okay. Thanks. I don't even remember that day. I'll have to think about that."

Ben nods his head. "The thing is that you are always so intense and never take a break. You barely go home at night. None of us want to work that hard."

Daniel decides to forego any further questions. Ben's comments have already given him enough to think about.

Daniel smiles at Ben. "Thanks Ben. Do you mind if I ask you a few more questions at a later time?"

"Sure." Ben stands up and leaves the office.

Daniel smiles as Ben leaves the office. *Ben's comments are so accurate,* he thought. *I wouldn't enjoy working for a boss like me, either. It felt good reconnecting with Ben. I've missed connecting with the group. How did I become so off-balance with getting results being the focus and friendship being ignored? Today is a new start!*

Daniel smiles again as he decides the first step in the new start is something fun for *his* weekend.

PART TWO

Connection To Others

Part Two of **The Leadership Energy Model** is Connection to Others. This section is probably the most comfortable area of discussion for those in the western culture. The bio-energy addition will add richness and depth to your leadership success.

Chapter Three: iAchieve
"I can accomplish both easy and difficult tasks with grace and ease."

Chapter Four: iCare
"I am completely loved and completely loveable."

Chapter Five: iSpeak
"I speak my truth and it is liberating."

CHAPTER THREE

iAchieve

"I can accomplish easy and difficult tasks with grace and ease."

IT IS TIME for Stephanie's review. She sits at a table across from her boss, Steve. The table is full of paper with numbers, notes, and data. There are many accolades from Steve. She is feeling content and proud of her work.

Steve asks a question, "So, Stephanie, where do you want to go with your career?"

"Well," she replies, "I would like to continue to work on the City of Albany project. We have the right people on the team and they seem to enjoy the work. I want to continue supporting the goals you have set for the project and the team."

Steve thinks for a moment and then asks, "Stephanie, everything you just told me is either about the project or what others want. What do YOU want?"

Stephanie sits in silence. She wonders, *what does he mean, what do I want?*

Finally, she answers, "I'm not sure what you mean."

"I thought so," Steve responds. "There are two things leaders need to do. They need to know where they want to go in their life and career AND they need to know where they want the team to go. You are very good at setting goals and achieving results based on what I need or the project needs. It's time to take the next step. It's time to define what YOU want from your career."

"Is something wrong with wanting to deliver results for you and the team?" asks Stephanie.

"Not at all," replies Steve. "But if you truly want to grow as a leader, then what I am suggesting will be important."

Stephanie puts her chin on her hand. With a puzzled look, she replies, "I'm not sure that I understand. Do you have an example?"

"I have something better in mind. If you're agreeable, I'd like to give you an assignment. Are you in?" asks Steve.

"Sure," replies Stephanie. She thought, *what do I have to lose?*

Steve continues. "I would like you to answer three questions and then we can talk about them next week. They are: What do you want from your career? What talents do you bring? And where do you want to go from here?"

Stephanie thought for a moment. She had no idea how to answer these questions. She slowly responds, "Okay…I'll give your suggestion a try."

"Great," Steve smiles. "I'll see you next week."

Stephanie's lack of clarity in her personal focus and direction is a symptom of the struggle in iAchieve energy. Personal focus and direction give power to achieve both personally and as a leader. The iAchieve energy gives the clarity, intention, and action to achieve results.

Any energy associated with achieving should be an easy energy source for the western culture mindset. However, the opposite is true. Think about your school experience. Were you allowed to determine the direction you desired? Or, were you taught to sit quietly while someone else defined for you the assignment and how results should be delivered? The assumption is, if you work hard, and do what others ask, you will gain power and recognition. I meet many leaders who have worked hard and it has not led to the progress they desired. You can only achieve if you move forward with clarity and intention. Let's look at the leadership competencies and energy ingredients that bring this concept to life.

The Leadership Competencies

Of the sixty-seven leadership competencies defined by the Lominger Institute, there are three we will discuss in the iAchieve category. They are: Career Ambition, Perseverance, and Managing Vision and Purpose.

Career Ambition starts with you. If you are open in iAchieve energy, you will know what you want from your career and actively move toward that goal. You will make things happen for yourself and not wait for others to create opportunities. It you are closed in iAchieve energy, you may make unwise career choices, be unsure of what you want from your career, or become stuck in a career or organization that is not a fit for your strengths and desires.

Perseverance is the energy and drive to finish things, especially in the face of resistance or setbacks. Closed iAchieve energy leaders either stick with things too long, or they give up too soon. In either case, goals and desires are not accomplished, causing distress in life and career.

The third area of iAchieve energy is Managing Vision and Purpose. Effective leaders are not only clear about vision and purpose for the organization, but also for their life and career. Leaders open in iAchieve energy communicate a compelling and inspiring vision, talk optimistically about possibilities and create mileposts to rally support behind their vision. Leaders with closed iAchieve energy leave people behind and lack support for their vision.

The Energy Ingredient

iTrust and iConnect energies are the foundation for iAchieve energy. If you trust who you are and the unique strengths you bring, plus you are confident in yourself, you can now begin to effectively move forward to achieve the visions and goals for your life. If you do not trust your unique strengths, you will struggle connecting with others and inspiring them to follow your lead.

The statement "I can accomplish easy and difficult tasks with grace and ease," implies a focus and an inspiration to tackle anything. If the iAchieve energy is open, there is a sense of your own power. Your vision, focus, and intention are a source of inspiration for you and others.

Let me give you an example. I worked with Mark several years ago. Mark was highly regarded in his organization. However, he was extremely frustrated in his career. He knew he could continue to be successful in his current position. But, he wanted something else, something more. When I asked what that was, he had a few vague ideas, but couldn't clearly answer the question.

We worked together focusing on the three questions: What do I want in my career? What talents do I bring? Where to from here? It was important that he wrote his thoughts down as we worked through several self-reflection exercises. Why writing? Our brain can only hold, process, and focus on a limited amount of information. Writing allows a person to see the bigger picture until clarity develops.

After several weeks, Mark was excited about the work he had done on the three questions. By answering the three questions, he became clear about his desired future direction. Now it was time to share it with others. Mark told me, "Cheryl, the future I have defined will never happen in my current organization without several people either retiring or dying!" I told him, while I hoped death was not the outcome, that he had nothing to lose by sharing this vision and purpose with a few key leaders.

Mark called four months later. "Cheryl, you'll never guess what happened." I responded, "Please don't tell me several people died!" Mark laughed and reported, "No, but there has been a re-organization and they have specifically designed a position to fit my vision and purpose. It would not have happened if I had not clearly communicated my desires." iAchieve energy in action!

According to bio-energy information, the physical location of the iAchieve energy is about three finger widths above the navel at the base of the rib cage. It is here that we expand the trust in ourselves and establish our ability to take action. Here lies our self-esteem, and personal power. In open iAchieve energy, we have the momentum to create our clarity of vision and purpose, and the fire to manifest our dreams. It is from this spot that we often describe "gut feelings" or the sense of knowing what needs to be done.

If the iAchieve energy is blocked, the emotional experience is guilt or lack of control. We may feel like a victim and powerless. We may give our power and dreams away just to keep peace in relationships. We may also experience physical symptoms such as stomachaches, anxiety, digestive disorders, diseases of the liver, pancreas or gallbladder.

Awareness Activities

Examine Your iAchieve Energy

Answer the following questions to examine the iAchieve energy in you.

» Are you clear about what you want from your career?

» Do you actively work to open doors to achieve your career goals?

» Do you focus and finish things even in the face of roadblocks or setbacks?

» Do you communicate the vision and purpose for your life and your career?

» Are you optimistic about the future?

» Do you create mileposts to rally support behind your vision and purpose?

The more you answer "yes" to the above questions, the stronger the indication that your iAchieve energy is open. Conversely, the more "no" answers indicate a need to open and expand iAchieve energy.

Developing Clarity of Vision

In Mark's story, I shared the concept of developing clarity of career vision. Here are five important tips to creating a personal vision.

1. Time: Determining your career vision and plan is not a "fast food" endeavor. In this era of speed, this is one area that requires your time and attention. Some people work intensively for several days and others spread the process out over several weeks. Either way, it takes time. The first step is to give yourself permission

and patience to take the time you need to create a vision and plan based on wisdom, not speed.

2. Awareness: The amount of time you need is directly related to your own awareness of your strengths, values, interests, personal style, and future goals. If you have not taken time to listen to yourself, or, if you are like most of us and have not thought about what to listen to, then you will need more time. Through the process of awareness comes the clarity of what you need, want, know, and desire.

3. Articulation: From awareness comes the next step, which is articulating our awareness. You need to understand and articulate what you know in the following areas:

    » Career Development: What you have learned from your past experiences that lead you to better choices. Observe patterns to what you enjoyed and what you didn't enjoy throughout your life. Include your childhood, your teenage years and your adult life.

    » Abilities: What comes natural and easy to you. The hardwiring of how you operate.

    » Skills: What you have learned. The software you have added to your knowledge base.

    » Interests: The things that bring you passion and enjoyment.

    » Personal Style: Your style, personality, temperament, and the environments you need to honor this style.

    » Beliefs: What beliefs you hold about success, career and achieving life fulfillment. Often these come from your family of origin. What beliefs help you move forward and what holds you back.

    » Values: Those guiding forces that are key to your life decisions.

    » Goals: What you want to achieve.

Understanding each of these factors is much like building a stir-fry. You need to take the time to chop the ingredients before you can begin to create the final product.

4. Integration: Pull together the ingredients from above into a vision and a plan to move forward. This "product" comes from you. There is not one expert in the world who can tell you what this needs to be. That is why you need the time and patience to listen to yourself. The result is a powerful, energizing, and unique creation that will move you forward to further career satisfaction and life fulfillment.

5. Experience: No matter how wise you are, evaluated experience is a great teacher. Life continues to move and you continue to integrate new experiences and knowledge into your wisdom. Unless you evaluate this new data and allow it to move your decisions and choices, the creation you developed in step four soon becomes stagnant. Take the time to evaluate, make new choices, and transform your future focus. This keeps the vision and plan powerful, energizing, and unique.

Other Suggestions

The following are activities that support the iAchieve energy. As with the previous lists, don't overanalyze the "why" and "how." I ask you to trust the eastern bio-energy research that supports the wisdom and selection of these activities.

- »   Yell out loud (in an appropriate place)
- »   Change your routine
- »   Rock climbing
- »   Hiking
- »   Build and watch a fire
- »   Ripping up boxes
- »   Laughing yoga

Action Learning

This action learning exercise focuses on the iAchieve energy. The physical location for the iAchieve energy is located above the navel at the base of your rib cage. The emotional energy that either opens, becomes blocked, or closes is centered in this area.

Before you begin, focus your awareness on this area. Suggestions to add focus include: holding your hand over this area, looking in the mirror specifically observing this area, or using a word or two to describe the feelings in this area before you begin.

Now it is time for you to work on these three questions: What do I want in my career? What talents do I bring? Where to from here?

1. This will be a writing exercise. Make sure you have plenty of paper!

2.   Review the list below and write down any ideas or thoughts you have as you think about each category. For example, begin with Career Development. What have you learned from past experiences that help you make better choices today? You might answer, "I like to work alone," or "I can't work in large organizations." Simply write down whatever comes to mind. You will want to review each item on the list. Take time to think and reflect but always write it down. No judgments. No right or wrong. Write it all down. Here is the list:

    » Career Development: What have you learned from your past experience that leads you to better choices. Observe patterns to what you enjoyed and what you didn't enjoy. Include your childhood, your teenage years and your adult life.

    » Abilities: What comes natural and easy to you. The hardwiring of how you operate.

    » Skills: What you have learned. The software you have added to your knowledge base.

    » Interests: The things that bring you passion and enjoyment.

» Personal Style: Your style, personality, temperament, and the environment you need to honor this style.

» Beliefs: What beliefs you hold about success, career, and achieving life fulfillment. Often these come from your family of origin. What beliefs move you forward and what beliefs hold you back.

» Values: Those guiding forces that are key to your life decisions.

» Goals: What you want to achieve.

3. Once you have completed brainstorming in all areas, gather three sheets of paper. On the first sheet, write the question on the top, "What do I want?" On the second sheet, write, "What do I bring?" And finally, on the third sheet, "Where to from here?'

4. Now review your list of brainstormed items. As you look at each item, decide under which question the item belongs. Think of these sheets as collection areas to gather relevant thoughts to each question. You may find an item that could fit under two of the questions. If so, put it in both spots. For example, "I like to be organized," might fit under what you want (e.g. an organized environment) and what you bring (e.g. I am organized).

5. Once you have sorted your thoughts under each question, now begin to write the answer to each question until it states what you want it to say. The items on each sheet of paper should guide you to write a statement or paragraph that honors who you are. Remember: No judgment. There is no right or wrong.

6. Your ultimate goal is to combine the answers to all three questions into a one-page document. Length is not the critical measurement; clarity is. This will be a document for you! Eventually, you may decide to share all or parts of this with others. But, most importantly, write the first version for you.

Stephanie Revisited

It has been a week since Steve gave Stephanie the assignment to work on the three questions: What do I want in my career? What talents do I bring? Where to from here? She had spent the week journaling about these questions and had no idea if she had done the exercise correctly. She is more comfortable thinking about what others want from her, not what she wants for herself. It had been a challenge, but not as difficult as she had first thought.

She sits down at Steve's office table. Steve greets her, "I can't wait to hear your answers."

"I don't know if I did this the way you wanted." Stephanie states nervously.

"You can't do it wrong," laughs Steve. "Unless you didn't do it! Why don't you share with me what you wrote? Let's start with 'what do you want?'"

"Okay," replies Stephanie. "I wrote down that I want to be in a supportive work environment. I want to work with a team who values the work as much as I do. I want to take projects from start to finish. I want to continue to take on new, challenging projects and be recognized for the work I do."

Steve nods his head as he encourages her to continue. "Okay. Go on to the next question. What talents do you bring?"

"Well, I think I am organized and I know how to collaborate with others. I enjoy building teams to focus on a project. I am an expert in our technologies and the process to get the work done. I am a hard worker." She feels confident as she shares this list.

Steve encourages her to continue. "And the next question 'Where to from here?'"

"That was the most difficult," replies Stephanie. "I don't know what's available."

"Yes, I can see where that would be a challenge. You've been so focused on your work that I would guess you don't make the time to network with other managers and directors," comments Steve.

Stephanie nods her head.

"Anything else on your list?" asks Steve.

"No, that's it," replies Stephanie.

"Okay, now let's go back to the first question. Based on your answers to what you want, is what you are currently doing meeting that criteria?" asks Steve.

Stephanie thinks for a few moments and then responds, "Yes, for the most part. I was disappointed to not continue on and complete the Holbrook project. But I can see where the opportunity to take on a challenging new project meant I needed to let go of Holbrook. Since I have just taken on the City of Albany, I think it will be awhile before I am ready to take on something else."

Steve laughs. "Okay. Great. We are on the right track. Let's talk about the what you bring list. This is a good list, but I think you should add that you not only collaborate with others, but you also have the trust and respect of both your peers and direct reports."

"Okay." Stephanie replies, as she writes the additional items on her list.

Steve continues. "Now let's talk about the last question, 'where to from here?' While it looks like you are on the right track with the City of Albany project, it never hurts to network with others and learn what opportunities might be on the horizon. Would you be okay if I set up meetings with Jack and Robin? Since they are the other two directors, I think they should know more about you."

Stephanie asks. "What would I talk about?"

"Take the opportunity to learn more about their projects. I will set up the email request letting them know I want them to meet you so you can learn more about their projects. They are used to these types of meetings. It won't be difficult. Just be ready to talk about your projects and possibly the answers to the questions we just discussed."

"I can do that. Anything else?" asks Stephanie.

"Yes. What did you think about this assignment?" asks Steve.

Stephanie thought for a moment and replied. "I thought it would be complicated, but it was easier than I thought."

Steve stands as they finish the meeting. "Great meeting, Steph. Let me know how the meetings go with Jack and Robin."

Stephanie walks back to her office. She feels calm, yet energized. She has never felt this way before. She is grateful to Steve for challenging her to think about her career focus and direction. It was the first time she had the support and process to develop her career focus. It was easier than she had expected. Perhaps, a new perspective on her life, her career and her success was about to unfold.

CHAPTER FOUR

iCare

"I am completely loved and completely loveable."

DANIEL SITS IN Julie's office. It has been three months since he took over the Manager's role. Julie, the Human Resource Director, has called a meeting to review how things are going with his employees. Four people have left the company since Daniel took over as Manager. The exit interviews had identified Daniel as the main reason for their decision to leave. They found Daniel as constantly driving productivity, giving little to no recognition for hard work, and, in general, claimed all fun in the workplace was gone.

Although Daniel did not like the feedback, he has made several changes and feels things are on track. Julie had recently talked to a few people in his department to see how things were going. Daniel anticipates hearing good things from Julie at today's meeting.

Julie begins, "Well Daniel, how are things going?"

"I think things are going much better," replies Daniel. "I met with Ben after we last spoke and he pointed out a few things to me. I've been working hard at smiling more and having a bit more fun with the team. It feels good!"

"That's a start," replies Julie. "As you know, I spoke with a few of your staff members and I think there are additional things you can do."

More work, thought Daniel. *Really, I already have too much to do.* He sat silently waiting for Julie to continue.

Julie looks Daniel in the eye. "I can tell you didn't like what I just said. Tell me what you are thinking."

"I guess it is the old Daniel meeting the new Daniel," he replies. "My first thought was 'really! You want me to do more work! I'm already up to my eyeballs managing several projects.' Then I realized that I need to listen and learn more so I can become the leader I want to be."

"I know you work hard," replies Julie. "I also want you to be the leader you want to be. I know I can help you get there. Let me ask you a few questions."

"Okay," says Daniel.

Julie starts, "Who would you say are your top two people?"

Without hesitation, Daniel states, "Amy and Scott."

"What can you tell me about what motivates Amy?" asks Julie.

Daniel doesn't know how to respond. After a long silence, Julie continues, "Okay. Skip Amy. What can you tell me about Scott?"

"He works hard...he likes big projects..." Daniel's voice wanders off. He is not sure how to answer the question.

"Okay," replies Julie. "How many times last week did Amy or Scott stop by your office to touch base or ask a question?"

Daniel realizes he is stumped by these questions. He slowly responds, "We have our weekly group meeting. Neither just stops by."

"Does anyone just stop by your office or stop you in the hallway to chat?" asks Julie.

"No. We're all too busy working." Daniel's frustration increases.

Julie doesn't want to push Daniel too far. "I'm trying to help you see that there is no relationship between even your strongest employees and you."

"Is that what they told you?" asks Daniel.

"Not specifically Amy or Scott. What I did hear from the people I spoke to is that you manage projects well and they have noticed you're working to be more positive," reports Julie.

Daniel interrupts, "Well, that's good!"

Julie continues, "Yes, that is good. They respect your knowledge and see you trying. What they don't see is your caring about them and their career. They feel more like a commodity than a person. As long as work is being delivered, they hear nothing. Does that make sense?"

Julie and Daniel sit in silence. Finally Daniel says, "So what do you want me to do?"

"I guess that's up to you. You can continue as you are or you can add a few new tools. I have some ideas that might help," offers Julie.

Daniel sighs. "I'm not sure what I will do, but I am willing to listen."

Julie spends the rest of the hour sharing ideas and tools for Daniel to consider. Daniel leaves the office feeling discouraged. He needs time to think and decide what his next step will be.

The Leadership Competencies

The iCare statement is "I am completely loved and completely loveable." You may have scratched your head or chuckled as you read that statement. Clients have looked at me in disbelief stating "Really? It's about love? Isn't that inappropriate in the workplace?" I am not talking about romantic love. iCare energy is expanding compassion and understanding toward others. Genuine caring and compassion will lead to stronger results as well as add a sense of community.

Let's start with understanding iCare energy through the lens of leadership competencies. As you recall, leadership competencies are the behaviors exhibited by effective leaders. In using Lominger Institutes Leadership competencies, there are three that fit the iCare energy. They are: Motivating Others, Approachability, and Caring About Direct Reports.

Motivating Others is the first competency. When iCare energy is open, leaders create a climate in which people want to do their best. Individuals feel important and their team respects the leader.

Leaders with closed iCare energy may be a person you avoid. These leaders often pick their favorite individuals, whom they are willing to invest in. They provide inequitable treatment among their reports and have a one-size-fits-all model of motivation. The closed iCare leaders, intentionally or unintentionally, demotivate others.

Approachability is another competency consistent with iCare energy. Open iCare leaders are easy to talk to as they spend extra time putting others at ease. They are good listeners, sensitive to and patient with the interpersonal anxieties of others. Closed iCare leaders are distant and hard to know. They may be tense and uncomfortable in interacting with others and avoid talking about themselves.

The final iCare competency is Caring About Direct Reports. The open iCare energy is interested in the work and non-work lives of their direct reports. They ask about their plans, problems, and desires. They monitor workload and appreciate extra effort. The closed iCare leader has two extremes.

» The leader who cares too much and has trouble being firm with others. They get too deep in the personal lives of others and don't allow the individuals to be accountable or successful. This suffocation damages others as much as the leader who does not care. By taking over the work or not allowing others to take on challenges, this leader sends the message "you are not competent."

» The leader who does not care about the personal needs of direct reports. They are either too busy to know much about others or may believe that work and personal lives should be separate.

Daniel is one example of closed iCare leadership. Nancy is another. Nancy cares too much about her direct reports and limits both their success and hers.

Nancy had been promoted because of high scores on employee surveys and her ability to motivate others to achieve results. What the organization doesn't know is the amount of work she does for others. Nancy works sixty to seventy hours a week. While she isn't physically at work accumulating these hours, she works late in the evening after her kids have gone to bed. Her direct reports think she is great because she never expects extended work hours from them. If anyone indicates they have plans for the weekend or kid's events at night, she takes from them whatever task needs completion, so they can enjoy their personal time.

This worked until she was promoted. With the expansion of responsibilities, it was impossible for her to keep up with all the work demands. She is frustrated and results are suffering. She could see no other option than to submit her resignation, convinced she could not do the job. Nancy's boss persuaded her to stay for three months. He promised to assist her in developing leadership tools to help delegate and hold others accountable. If, after three months, Nancy still wanted to leave, he would support her decision and assist her in finding a new position.

The next three months were a challenging time for Nancy. If she wasn't doing the work for others, she had no idea on how to be a leader. She worried people would not like her or perform their work at the level needed.

Nancy began using a goal setting process to assist her with holding others accountable. As Nancy assigns tasks to others, she uses the following list.

- » Goal for the task
- » Rewards of completing the task
- » Consequences of not completing the task
- » Possible obstacles
- » Solutions to the obstacles
- » Necessary action steps
- » Date of completion
- » Delegated to
- » Target Date
- » Today's date

Nancy used this process, not only for delegating to others, but also for setting her own goals. Her biggest obstacle was herself. Her taking on the work of others needed to change. She was able to identify the following solutions: setting clear goals with others, allowing others to assume the responsibilities, and consistent follow-up to ensure results were achieved.

She is now ready to delegate tasks to others. With the employee identifying their rewards, consequences, obstacles, and solutions to their obstacles, the employee was able to take responsibility and accountability for the task assigned. Nancy was able to develop confidence that the individual was as invested as she was. It was reassuring to her that the employee could identify their own obstacles and determine solutions. She said, "How silly of me to believe that others can't take charge of their work!"

At the end of three months, Nancy was encouraged by the changes in herself and others. Employee surveys remained strong. Results were being delivered without working excessive hours. The struggle for Nancy was her life outside of work. Work had become an excuse for her to ignore her personal goals and satisfaction. She decided to stay with the company. The new goal for herself is to determine what she needed to fulfill her life.

The Energy Ingredient

In bio-energy studies, love is a mindset, a way of living versus a behavior. It is the passion and self-acceptance or yourself and others without conditions. The open iCare energy is a balance between giving and receiving. It is the willingness to not only give love and caring, but also to receive love and caring from others.

iCare energy is a very vulnerable energy. You may have very open iCare energy until you experience a death, a bad relationship, or someone letting you down. It is a natural reaction to close iCare energy when you feel hurt. Protecting yourself is important. Caring for the hurt is important. However, when you permanently close or create blocks in iCare energy, your life, your career and your joy will be significantly impacted.

The iCare energy template is located in the center of your chest. When you make the statement "It broke my heart," you are describing an event that is experienced in the iCare energy dimension. Hurt, disappointment in relationships, and perceived rejection are factors that contribute to closed iCare energy. Eastern philosophies identify the physical symptoms associated with closed iCare energy: heart issues, lung issues, allergies, asthma, breast disorders, circulatory problems, and shoulder, arm or hand issues.

Awareness Activities

Forgiveness

Dr. Beatrice Berry author of *I'm On My Way but Your Foot is On My Head*, states, "Forgiveness is not letting someone off the hook, it is getting off the hook they put you on." Who do you need to forgive? Why? While the other person may have hurt you, you also played a role in that relationship. What role did you play? What do you need to forgive about yourself?

Consider Linda. Linda accepted a position with a new company. She has been at the company for three weeks and realizes this was a bad decision. Her co-workers are unwelcoming and barely speak to her. She is quickly thrown into work with little to no support or direction. When she asks to meet with her manager, he is too busy and is told to figure it out on her own. Over the next eighteen months, she continually feels rejected. This did not bring out her best qualities. She becomes sarcastic and closes any efforts to build relationships with her co-workers. She loses her optimistic spark and often feels she needs to guard and protect herself. She finally decides to leave the organization.

For the next two years, she becomes angry every time she thinks of this experience. While she has moved to a new and more accepting position, the emotional impact of the previous position remains. As she speaks of this, I ask her about forgiveness. She replies, "Those guys! What jerks! Why should I forgive them?" I then ask about forgiving herself and she begins to cry. "I should have known better. There were so many signs during the interview. I should not have stayed so long." She has a long list of what she "should" have done. For the next several weeks we focus on activities to forgive herself. As anger and sadness toward herself subsides, so does the anger toward her former employer.

Linda's story is an example of "letting herself off the hook." Lack of forgiveness toward self is often the underlying issue with closed iCare energy. When you are giving too much to others, you are often doing so because you feel inadequate and need to make up for something. When you refuse to give to others, you are often protecting yourself from making another mistake. In either case, you cannot open the iCare energy without first forgiving yourself.

Gratitude

To strengthen iCare energy, you also need gratitude. The definition of gratitude is "the quality of being thankful; readiness to show appreciation for and to return kindness." In our western culture, you can become so consumed with *busy…busy…busy* that you miss the experiences of life. You miss the opportunity to find the connections that give you joy. Stopping throughout the day to observe and be thankful are simple tools to stay attuned to iCare energy. How many times have you stopped today and said, "Right now, I am thankful for…"

Other Suggestions

Here is the list of additional activities to further expand your iCare energy.

- » Write thank you notes
- » Own a pet
- » Give away your last bite
- » Read your past journals (have compassion for who you are)
- » Hand massage
- » Look in the mirror and state what you are thankful for about you

Action learning

This action learning exercise focuses on the iCare energy. As you work on the iCare energy, it is important to focus on the area in your body that houses this energy. For the iCare energy, this is located in the center of your chest. The emotional energy that either opens, becomes blocked, or closes is centered in this area.

Before you begin, focus your awareness on the center of your chest. Suggestions to add focus include: holding your hand over this area, looking in the mirror specifically observing this area, or using a word or two to describe the feelings in this area before you begin.

The action learning exercises center around forgiveness and gratitude.

Exercise #1: Forgiveness

1. Identify a person or event that continues to cause you hurt or rejection. It may be recent or something in the past.

2. Journal about this event using the following format:

   » Write in detail about what happened.

   » Why do you think this caused you hurt or rejection?

   » How do you feel about this situation *right now*? Write about your feelings at the time you are doing this exercise.

   » What or who can you forgive *right now*? Don't worry about who or what you *should* forgive. Write about what you *can* forgive *right now*. If the answer is nothing, that is fine. Be honest with yourself.

3. Don't force the responses. One word is fine. Be honest.

4. Once you are done, set the journal aside. Mark your calendar to revisit this journal in one week.

5. When you return to your journal, answer the same questions regarding the event. Approach this as if you had never written about this before.

6. Continue this process until your writing indicates you have forgiven yourself, the situation and the parties involved. What will be the sign? You may feel bored with the issue or you have completed what you need.

7. When you reach the completion stage, state out loud, "I am complete with this situation and I have forgiven myself, the situation and all parties involved.

Exercise #2: Gratitude

The goal of this exercise is to build the practice of gratitude into your daily life.

1. Think about your typical day. Are there recurring events that happen during your day? Here are a few examples:

   » Traveling by car to client meetings every day.

   » Having several meetings away from your office every day.

   » Brushing your teeth twice a day.

   The activity itself is not important. The important element is that you experience it as a daily event.

2. You will now create the trigger connection to cause a gratitude moment. When this event occurs is when you will identify what you are grateful at that moment. Here are a few examples:

   » You travel by car to client meetings each day. Your trigger event will be stopping at a stoplight. Each time you stop at a stoplight you will ask yourself "What am I grateful for *at this moment*?" Answer the question and continue on with your day.

   » You have a day full of meetings outside your office every day. Your trigger event will be walking to the meeting. Each time you walk to a meeting you will ask yourself

"What am I grateful for *at this moment*?" Answer the question and continue on with your day.

» You brush your teeth twice a day. Putting toothpaste on the toothbrush will be your trigger moment. Each time you put toothpaste on your toothbrush you will ask yourself "What am I grateful for *at this moment*?" Answer the question and continue on with your day.

3. That's it! Stay committed to this practice and notice what happens to you and your iCare energy.

Daniel revisited

Daniel has had time to think and decide his next steps with his team. He appreciates that Julie, the HR Director, has provided tools and ideas. One of the suggestions was to meet with each employee and learn about their background and career goals. Julie also provided a series of questions to guide the discussion. Daniel decides it is time to call another meeting with Ben.

Ben arrives promptly at 9:00 and the discussion begins.

Daniel greets Ben. "Thanks, Ben, for your time. I bet you are wondering why we are meeting?"

"Yeah. I'm guessing there is something you need with the bridge project," replies Ben.

Daniel responds. "Actually, no. Things are going fine on the bridge project. I wanted to spend time talking about you and your career."

Ben's anxiety is obvious as he shifts in his chair and looks toward the door.

Daniel chuckles, "Just relax. This is actually a follow-up conversation to several months ago when we discussed my style and need to have more fun in the workplace. Remember?"

"Yeah..." Ben is still visibly uncertain as to where this is going.

Daniel continues to smile, hoping it will put Ben at ease. "Well, Julie has given me a few suggestions and, since you were willing to give me feedback before, I thought you might be willing to help me again."

"Okay. Sure wish you had let me know before the meeting," replies Ben.

"Oh, I never thought of that. Guess I have a lot to learn." Daniel smiles and continues. "Are you okay with trying this out?"

Ben sits back in his chair and says, "Okay. Sure"

"Great. Let's start with you telling me about your career. I know you were someplace else before coming here. Fill me in," Daniel sits back in his chair.

Daniel spends the next hour listening to Ben talk about his career and his life. He asks questions from Julie's list including: what does Ben like about his job, what he doesn't he like about his job, and what he hopes to do in the future.

As the hour comes to an end, Daniel says, "Ben, we are almost out of time. I learned a lot today."

Ben stands up and pauses before he opens the door. "Daniel, it was great to talk again. Feels a bit like old times." Ben opens the door and leaves the office.

Daniel is pleased with the meeting and decides he is going to have similar conversations with each of his team members. Daniel thinks about what he learned from the conversation with Ben. First, he needs to let people know why they are meeting with him before the meeting. It is his job to create a comfortable conversation. Setting the meeting agenda will help. Daniel smiles as he realizes the second lesson he learned today. He really does want to be a leader who cares about others and takes the time to make a personal connection. Time to schedule meetings with Amy and Scott...

CHAPTER FIVE

iSpeak

"I speak my truth and it is liberating."

STEPHANIE IS IN the middle of a meeting with Doris. She has been dreading this meeting all week. Doris has been employed with the company for twelve years and has a very negative attitude. People avoid Doris because of how difficult she is to work with. Unfortunately, she has been allowed to continue this behavior without any consequences. Doris is a technical expert. Stephanie and the previous manager have always worked around Doris' attitude and its impact on the department because it would be hard to lose her technical knowledge. That strategy had worked until the City of Albany project. Now, three of the team members have come to Stephanie, complaining about how difficult Doris is to work with and, more importantly, how this was slowing down their productivity. Stephanie is doing her best to help Doris understand how her behavior is affecting others.

"So, you're saying I'm a problem," says Doris.

"Your technical work is fine but your attitude needs to change," replies Stephanie.

Doris crosses her arms and looks defiantly at Stephanie.

Stephanie continues. "I want to see what we can do to support you in changing."

Doris breaks her silence. "So what you're saying is you want me to change yet no one else has to! What about Rick. He's always lying about what I do."

Stephanie sighs. This is what happens when she talks with Doris— Doris blames someone else and ultimately, nothing happens. Stephanie has no idea what to do now. She doesn't want to push things too far and lose Doris just when she is most needed on the project. Yet, Doris is not going to be reasonable and see the wisdom of changing her ways.

Doris interrupts Stephanie's thoughts and says, "I've got to go. I have a meeting with Tara and I'm already late."

"Okay. We'll continue this discussion later. I'll schedule something on your calendar," replies Stephanie.

Doris leaves the office with a smile on her face. "Darn it!" thought Stephanie. "Doris has won again."

The Energy Ingredient

How do you express yourself? Do you know what you want to say in an honest, yet tactful, way? Do you have the courage to say what you need and want to say? Let's start the iSpeak discussion with the energy dynamic.

You often hear the saying "walk the talk." That is the outcome of open iSpeak energy; you speak the truth and others hear what you have to say. You are honest in your communication, which leads to a sense of understanding for both you and the listener.

If we are able to "walk the talk", we are in alignment with who we are and what we say. So imagine there is something that you want to say, but are fearful of losing your job or a relationship through your honesty. What happens to you? Clients report that they feel fear, anxiety, and the need to censor themselves. If you recall, fear is found in the iTrust energy. If you are feeling fearful, you will inhibit what you want to say, thus limiting the iSpeak energy.

Fear is one of the factors that inhibit iSpeak energy. Lies and secrets are additional factors that inhibit iSpeak energy.

Secrets create an environment in which you are not allowed to tell what you know to be true. If you are raised in an environment of lies and secrets, the iSpeak energy is closed early in your life. Or, you have open iSpeak energy in your home environment, but experience a situation or environment that includes lies and secrets. For example, a culture that is filled with gossip and in-direct communication can cause this energy to close or, at the very least, become censored.

We often think of leadership communication as communication to direct reports or followers. What about communication to your boss or senior leadership? The person or the situation can impact the iSpeak energy.

Let me tell you about Kathy. Kathy is an in-house attorney with five direct reports. As the company grows, the expectation is for Kathy to effectively delegate to her direct reports and create greater accountability for results. Kathy recognizes the need to grow in these areas and welcomes the opportunity to expand her leadership competency.

Kathy made tremendous progress over a two-month period. As she implemented her delegation and accountability skills, it became clear that Doug, her boss, was not as accountable to deliver results as he expected his team to be. Doug was slow to deliver needed information on time. He would promise to complete tasks but needed constant reminders and often missed due dates. This, in turn, slowed the progress of Kathy's team. It was now time for Kathy to practice accountability skills with Doug.

Kathy asked me to join the meeting with Doug. She is to conduct the meeting and I am there to support the progress. Kathy prepared the meeting agenda, just as she did with her direct reports, using the following outline.

- » What is the issue?
- » Goal for the meeting
- » Solutions the other person proposes
- » Solutions she proposes
- » Agreed solution—specific, measurable

» Potential obstacles

» Solutions to address these obstacles

» Date for follow-up

We reviewed her notes prior to the meeting. She was ready!

The meeting begins and Kathy introduces the issues and goals for the meeting. She is visibly nervous and not as clear as she had been in our preparation meeting. Doug begins to talk about his plans for the department, the growth of the company, and Kathy's progress with her direct reports. None of these topics relate to Kathy's goals for the meeting. Kathy remains quiet. I interrupt and move the conversation back to the agenda Kathy has prepared. She looks at me with fear in her eyes as she follows my lead to shift the conversation back to the agenda. The meeting concludes with Doug having some understanding of the issue but no defined action items.

As we debrief the meeting, Kathy recognizes how difficult it was for her to have direct, honest communication with Doug. It isn't Doug per se; it is her fear over the power he holds. Because of her fear, pleasing him is important. She works to avoid conflict at all costs.

Over the next two months, Kathy works to expand her managerial courage, and to have direct, honest, and tactful conversations with Doug. She recognizes that conversations "up" require greater preparation, courage, and focus on the agenda. One of the exercises she uses to prepare for her meetings with Doug is the grounding exercise from Chapter One—iTrust. Here is the exercise:

» Feel your feet on the ground.

» Take a breath focusing on the physical sensation of your feet on the ground.

» Now ask yourself, "What is my value *right now*?" The past does not dictate the future. The future cannot solve the present. What is your value *right now*?

» Now you are ready to speak your message.

As with all other energies, there is a physical dynamic for this energy. The physical energy center for iSpeak is in the hollow of your throat. The physical symptoms consistent with closed iSpeak energy include neck problems, jaw problems, thyroid issues, chronic sinus problems, or swollen glands in your throat.

The Leadership Competencies

What does iSpeak energy look like for an effective leader? Let me share a quote from Lynn Baskfield, Founder of *Wisdom Horse Coaching*. "When the dominant (leader) came over and tried to herd her, all she did was twitch an ear and he backed off. No fuss or fluster. Her grounded energy and clear communication completely engaged him, and also took his attention away from stirring up others, freeing them to interact more peacefully and cooperatively."

Lynn's quote is about a horse. The horse she describes is not the dominant leader. The dominant leader "did" things that gave the impression of being a leader. The horse Lynn describes is able to engage and communicate without being the dominant leader. They take charge in a subtle, yet powerful, way. Lynn adds to her description of the horse by saying, "(she) conserved energy while staying present."

Obviously, we are not horses! But, observing the leadership behavior of horses gives us clues as to how we can use iSpeak energy. It is not about how much we speak. It is not always about verbal communication. It is about being present, recognizing what needs to happen, and choosing the communication action necessary for you and your audience.

As you review the leadership competencies, you will see the direct impact of iSpeak energies on these competencies. Leaders need clear and open iSpeak energy to assist in focus, direction and results. From the sixty-seven Lominger Career Architect Leadership Competencies, there are two competencies to discuss: Managerial Courage and Informing Others.

Open iSpeak leaders show Managerial Courage by not holding back anything that needs to be said. They provide current, direct, complete, actionable, positive, and corrective feedback to others. People problems are faced quickly and directly. This does not mean they are unkind or abrasive. Rather, they are honest and ensure understanding. It is not about the quantity of words; it is about the quality of interactions.

Closed iSpeak leaders struggle to take a tough stand with others. They hold back in challenging feedback situations. Avoiding conflict is the goal, as they are afraid they may be wrong or may not be liked. This leader talks too much, rather than listening and responding to what is needed.

The leader with open iSpeak energy is competent in Informing Others. They establish clear direction, maintain two-way dialogue with others, and are a clear communicator. Information is provided to assist people with doing their jobs. They are honest and clear.

When leaders are clear with their iSpeak energy they are able to speak honestly, and it is liberating for all concerned. Even if it is tough information for the listener to hear, both parties are able to move forward for more effective solutions and results.

Awareness Activities

Activities to support open iSpeak energy include:

- » Honest and uncensored writing in a journal
- » Reading out loud or being read to
- » Neck rolls
- » Practicing silence
- » Pressing your palms to your ears

Action Learning

This action learning exercise focuses on the iSpeak energy. As I have mentioned in the other action learning exercises, it is important to focus on the area in your body that houses this energy. For the iSpeak energy, this is located in the hollow of your throat.

There are two exercises for iSpeak energy. The first exercise is clarifying what you want to say. The second exercise assists in developing the courage to speak your message.

Exercise #1: What do you want to say?

Journaling is the fastest way to open iSpeak energy. You need to understand what you *want* to say and have the opportunity to edit it until it accurately reflects what you *will* say.

» Start with a blank piece of paper. At the top write, "what do I *want* to say?" Write down everything that comes to your mind. Be honest. Don't censor a thing.

» After you have completed all the things you "*want* to say", now it is time to prepare what you *will* say. Take a second sheet of paper and write, "What I *will* say" on the top. Review the "*want* to say" items and transfer any items you believe you "*will* say" to this new sheet.

» Several things might happen as you prepare the "What I *will* say" sheet:

» You may have nothing you want to transfer. This is an indication that you may be fearful and need the courage to address the fear. If this is the case, you will want to go back to the Action Learning Exercise in Chapter One—iTrust.

» You may have several items that you transfer to the "*will* say" sheet. This is the beginning of your outline for the conversation that will need to occur. Before you leave the list, ask yourself, "Is there anything I need to put on the "*will* say" list that I am avoiding because I am fearful?" If so, put this on the list.

Exercise #2: Speaking It Out Loud

Once you understand what you want to say through journaling, it is time to say it out loud. You need to hear your voice speaking the words that are right for you.

1. Take the list of "what I *will* say."

2. Find a place to speak it out loud.

3. Speak it out loud a minimum of three times. You will notice

the change in words or tone as you edit "what I *will* say." You may need more than three times to speak it out loud. Use your judgment in determining what is right for you.

4. There may be items you have on the "What I *will* say" list that you are fearful of saying. During your practice, include these items and speak them out loud. One of three things will happen:

 » You become more comfortable with speaking these

 » You edit the items to make them easier

 » You decide to leave them out.

5. Schedule a time to speak to the person you wish to address.

6. Before the meeting, focus on the grounding exercise from Chapter One—iTrust. Here is the exercise:

 » Feel your feet on the ground.

 » Take a breath focusing on the physical sensation of your feet on the ground.

 » Now ask yourself, "What is my value *right now*?" The past does not dictate the future. The future cannot solve the present. What is your value *right now*?

7. You are now ready to speak the message! Are you nervous? That's normal and completely okay! You have done everything you need to prepare. You can do no more. Feel the nervousness, but don't let it stop you. Now go forth and do what you have worked so hard to make happen.

Stephanie revisited

Doris enters Stephanie's office with a scowl on her face. As promised, Stephanie has scheduled another meeting to discuss Doris' attitude and its impact on the team. Stephanie has done her homework and this time she is ready.

Stephanie begins, "Hi Doris. As you know, this is the follow-up meeting to our discussion last week about your relationships with other team members."

Doris nods her head and remains silent. Stephanie continues, "The goal of this meeting is to develop a plan."

Doris finally speaks, "Okay, what do you want me to do?"

"I am wondering if you have any ideas," asks Stephanie.

"Nope," replies Doris. "Since you chose to believe everyone else and not me, I don't see the point in my suggesting anything."

"I understand that you don't feel heard," states Stephanie. "And that you think others may be the problem."

"You bet!" says Doris. "Like I said last week, Rick is always lying about what I do. You should be talking to Rick, not to me!"

Stephanie responds, "That may happen, but today's meeting is about your behavior."

"Okay. So what do you want me to do?" asks Doris.

"First, let's make sure we both understand what people are concerned about." says Stephanie.

Doris's voice rises, "I'm busy! I don't have time to listen to their whining. You keep piling on more projects for me to do. I'm already stressed and all they do is create more stress!"

Stephanie knows she needs to keep her voice slow and steady to avoid the conversation escalating further. Even though Stephanie is feeling her own anxiety increase, it is important that she keep calm.

"I understand Doris," replies Stephanie. "I do ask a lot of you. You are very skilled in what you do and an important element in our projects. I think we can work together to see if we can find a way to decrease your work load."

Doris sighs.

Stephanie continues, "What I propose is that we schedule a weekly meeting to review your work priorities."

Doris challenges, "It might result in hiring a contractor or even another staff person."

"We can determine that when we meet," states Stephanie. She is determined to stay on her agenda and not be diverted onto other topics. "In the meantime, while we work on that, I need you to change how you treat others."

Doris sighs, "Like what?"

"For starters, you can't yell at others. When they come to you with a request, you need to listen to what they have to say. Your immediate response cannot be 'no'. If it is too much to fit into your schedule, you are to talk to me and we will decide what to do." Stephanie waits for Doris's reply.

After a short silence, Doris says, "You're going to work with me to decide what projects I should take on?"

"Yes," replies Stephanie. "I want us to have a set meeting every week, but if something comes up that needs to be discussed between meetings, I'll make myself available."

"Hmmm...okay...I guess we can see how that works," says Doris.

Stephanie recaps their conversation. "We've agreed so far on weekly meetings to review your work schedule and on my being available to review additional requests that surface. You've agreed to stop yelling at people. You've also agreed to completely listen to their requests and not respond with 'no' until we've reviewed it. Is that what you understand?"

Doris nods and stands up to leave. Stephanie stops her. "Wait Doris, we're not done."

Doris sits down. "What else?"

"Well, we need to talk about how you're going to deal with your frustration when people come to you. Agreeing to it and doing it are two separate things," replies Stephanie.

Doris laughs. "If you can solve that one, then my family will be delighted."

Stephanie chuckles. "What do you think you could do?"

Doris pauses before she speaks. "I'll have to think about that."

"Okay. We can talk more about this at our next meeting but remember, you agreed to stop yelling," states Stephanie. Stephanie was determined that Doris knew this was not going away.

"Let's schedule our weekly meeting for 8 AM on Fridays. Will that work?" asks Stephanie.

"It should," replies Doris.

"Anything else?" asks Stephanie.

"Nope. See you Friday," states Doris.

Doris leaves the office. Stephanie closes the door and stretches her neck. She can feel the tension that had built up during that meeting. She is pleased with what had happened. She knows these conversations would always be tension-filled and would require her to have a well thought out plan. Today, the plan worked!

PART THREE
Seeing The Big Picture

Seeing the big picture allows you to lead toward the future. Intuition expands as you open up these dynamic energy sources.

Chapter Six: iSee
'I see my life becoming more enjoyable with each new day."

Chapter Seven: iUnderstand
"I understand my purpose is larger than me."

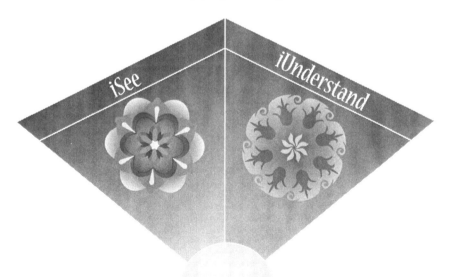

CHAPTER SIX

iSee

"I see my life becoming more enjoyable with each new day."

DANIEL IS SEATED on a plane flying home from the Varde project. It has been a good week. He finally has some time to think.

He has been in his role as Manager of the department for nine months. What a challenging time! He now knows the meaning of the statement, "The more I learn, the less I know."

His thoughts drift back to the events that have occurred over the past few months. His challenges began with people leaving because of his management style. He felt pressure from human resources to change. Next came the struggle with his team to deliver accurate results. Not knowing why people left and trying to train new people during a challenging time, it was all he could do to keep up. And, of course, there were problems created by things going out quickly, but not accurately. His boss had to smooth things over with several customers. He had never felt so unsure in his life!

Last week, his boss asked him if he was willing to do what it would take to be successful in leading the department. Daniel admitted the question took him by surprise. He answered "yes" but it caused him to stop and think. He did want the role, but he realized how different the responsibilities were now than in his previous position. What kind of leader did he want to be? How would he engage others to work with him? What would he need to change to become the leader he wanted to be? There was a great deal to think about.

Well, Daniel, he said to himself. *It's time to figure out the answers. Put up or shut up!*

It is late. It has been a busy week. He has no desire to answer these questions now. He makes a note of the questions he needs to answer. Then he closes his eyes for a nap.

The Leadership Competencies

The third section of **The Leadership Energy Model** includes iSee and iUnderstand energies. These areas are distinctly different from the previous energy discussions. Seeing The Big Picture requires going beyond delivering work and managing outcomes to a larger perspective of how and what you want to be as a leader.

In Janet Hagberg's book, *Real Power: Stages of Personal Power in Organizations,* she describes the transition as moving from building your ego to letting go of your ego. It is an interesting paradox. You spend your early career building credibility and recognition for your individual efforts and results. You then progress to a leadership level where you need to let go of your personal recognition in order to lead through others. Leadership is inspiring others to work toward your aspirations. This requires giving up personal control, while trusting and inspiring others to take over what has been so important to you for such a long time.

Janet Hagberg's model of Personal Power describes six stages of leadership development. Her fourth stage is the "Power by Reflection". She describes this as the "sandwich stage." This is a time when leaders face their fear of letting go of control. They become comfortable with their personal style. They show honesty, fairness, sound judgment, and follow through. They become competent in collaboration and enjoy mentoring others. They inspire others to hope and trust.

As a component of moving to this fourth stage, Janet Hagberg describes "the wall." Although an individual may have a vision and plan for him or herself, this is the first time they ask "why?" "Why do I want this power?" "Am I doing what I really want to be doing?" Some leaders hit the wall and choose not to address these questions. For those leaders, they will be limited in seeing the big picture. Are there leaders who can lead without seeing the big picture? Yes. These leaders remain operational in nature, focusing on managing results and delivering work.

Leaders who are able to move past "the wall" demonstrate three leadership competencies consistent with open iSee energy. The three leadership competencies are Perspective, Dealing with Ambiguity, and Innovation Management. These leaders are able to look toward the broadest view of an issue or situation. They effectively cope with change and make decisions without having the total picture. They are not upset when things are up in the air. They have a faith, which evolves into answers, and are open to exploring innovative ideas. They encourage creative ideas, both in themselves and others, and they are able to bring these ideas to reality.

Conversely, leaders who have closed iSee energy have a narrow view of issues and challenges. They struggle with change and uncertainty and prefer the tried and true. Innovation and new ideas are not welcome in their leadership role.

Let me tell you about Jack. Jack was a leader who believed he would never be able to lead through change. He was an engineer who valued the tried and true. As a project manager, he was a strong leader in delivering results through others. He enjoyed his work and received recognition for the results his team delivered.

Then his world changed. His company was purchased. The new company culture encouraged change and innovation. Jack doubted his ability to work with this new culture. Would he be able to shift his leadership? His response was always, "I don't know." My response back to him was, "What would you know if you did know?" This question is targeted to open iSee energy and the exploration of issues beyond the obvious tried and true solutions.

The first assignment from the new organization was to identify the most challenging client, then to brainstorm what changes needed to happen to be of greater value to that client. Jack's most challenging client was constantly demanding more services without any increase in fees. Jack could push the issue and force the client to pay more or limit their services, but this client was thirty percent of the profitable revenue for his group. The solutions were not easy or obvious.

When we began to discuss how Jack would approach this assignment, he began with the usual response of, "I don't know what we need to do." And my usual response was, "What would you know if you did know?" This was always met with a scowl. Jack identified that he was not going to be the one to find quick solutions for this assignment. This was a challenge for Jack. He liked to be in control and have the answers. We then began to discuss how his team might play a role in providing the answers. We clarified the issues surrounding this client and the list of questions he could bring to his team.

Jack discovered leadership at the iSee energy level. This leadership was not about doing more or knowing more. This level of leadership was about enrolling others while you facilitate the process. It is not about having all the answers. It is allowing the questions to bring solutions from others.

For Jack, he needed to play to his strength of delivering results. Once he could remove himself as the source of the answers and shift his role from, "expert with the answers," to "facilitator of the discussion," he became a stronger leader and found greater satisfaction for himself and his team. By bringing the question to his team, those employees with strength in generating ideas could shine. Once ideas were generated and everyone agreed upon solutions, Jack's strength in delivering results would re-enter the process. If his ego said, "I need to have the answers," then doubt emerged. Once he allowed himself to facilitate others who could contribute to the answers, success as a leader was realized.

The Energy Perspective

The iSee energy is not about eyesight. It is about intuition. What is intuition? Does the definition roll off your tongue? Or do you "know it when you see it".

Webster's definition of intuition is the "ability to understand something without the need for conscious reasoning." The challenge with this definition is, if conscious reasoning is not involved, then how do you teach someone intuition? Therein lies the challenge as I discuss this area of energy perspective. If this is new information, you will need to expand your acceptance of new, non-linear information in order to open the iSee perspective.

In Carol Tuttle's *Chakra 7* training, she describes this shift. "The shift is from using the logical mind to making survival decisions to opening your intuitive knowing to guide your life to abundance." The iSee energy is knowing what is needed. Have you ever done something and you knew it was the right thing to do? Yet, when someone asks you why you did it, you cannot come up with a cohesive, logical response. You finally say, "It was just the right thing to do." That is iSee energy in action.

The element that closes iSee energy is doubt. When you doubt yourself you close iSee energy. This is a bit different than iTrust energy, which shuts down because of a fear that you can't perform. In iSee energy, you know you can perform, and have set the course to proceed forward. You begin moving forward but doubt stops or limits you.

Where does doubt come from? There are several sources of doubt. First is a reaction from others to our intuitive responses. Intuition is present in all of us. Intuition grows with experience and reinforcement. So, if you begin to use your intuition at a young age and others laugh or do not listen, you would be taught to doubt or ignore your intuition.

The second reason iSee energy becomes closed or blocked is when you feel the need to have acceptance from others. iSee energy is your own Personal Guidance System. If you check with others to see if your intuition is "right," you will not always receive the reinforcing feedback you need, so you shut down the intuitive iSee energy.

A good example is the writing of this book. The concept of writing this book came ten months before I actually began writing. It was not a logical decision. It came to me while I was busy doing something else. Within two days of the intuitive idea, I had the book outlined. With excitement, I began to share the book concept with others. The puzzled looks, the listening but not understanding, and the silent nods led me to doubt the idea and put it aside.

The beauty of iSee energy is when your intuition speaks it demands to be heard! I would "stumble" across my outline while working on other things. Content and stories for this book would frequently enter my thoughts. I would find myself talking about it, even though I knew the responses might not always result in support. It was clear that I needed to act on my intuition knowing that this was the right direction. My Personal Guidance System took over. I continued to talk with others about the book. Not for their approval, but as a declaration to myself that this book was going to happen! The fact that you are now holding it in your hands is the evidence that intuitive iSee energy, while not logical, is certainly a powerful force.

How many times does your intuition know the right thing to do, but you shut it down because of the reactions from others? When you stop listening to your intuition, you become conditioned to no longer hear your intuitive messages.

David is a great example of closed iSee energy. When I met David, he was forty-eight years old and had worked in sales or sales management for a Fortune 500 company for most of his career. Our coaching work was focused on his leadership. However, during one of our conversations, he made a comment that he had always wanted to own a winery in California. Not being able to resist, I asked him to tell me more about this. He had dreamed of owning a winery since high school. He described in detail the winery, his workday, and his family living at this imagined winery. His family had laughed at him when he first voiced this as a teenager. He had written it off as a silly teenage dream. But, here he was 30 years later describing in detail this "silly teenage dream".

Over the course of our work together, he continued to expand his leadership success. While the winery dream was not directly related to his leadership, it was directly related to him. I encouraged him to write more about this dream and, even if it hadn't happened earlier in his life, to write what would happen if it occurred now. His dream began to come alive. His kids were in college, so he knew he had five years where his current income and location were important. The reality of owning a winery, with a five-year timeline of preparation, began to take place.

It has been eight years since I worked with David. The last I heard from him, he was a partner in a California winery. He had the opportunity to take an early retirement from his sales manager role. This created an opportunity to see if the winery option could come to fruition. And it did. The difference between logical, conscious reasoning and intuition is time. Logical, conscious reasoning implies a time line with outcomes. Intuition implies a knowing with the flexibility to respond as the opportunities occur. What a challenge to our western thinking!

The iSee energy is located in your forehead between your eyes. You might have heard the term "third eye" as a description of this intuitive energy portal. It is the source of self-reflection, discernment, and intuition. Physical symptoms of blocked or closed iSee energy are headaches, upper and frontal sinus conditions, neurological disturbances and eyesight issues.

Awareness Activities

Activities to support iSee energy include:

» Dream journaling—write your dreams down first thing in the morning. What are they telling you?

» Visualization—visualize an event as you wish it to be

» Guided imagery

» Drawing and painting

» Watching the sunrise and the sunset.

Action Learning

The emotional energy that opens, becomes blocked, or closes iSee energy is centered between your eyes. Before you begin the action learning exercise, focus your awareness on this area. Suggestions to add focus include: holding your hand over this area, looking in the mirror specifically observing this area, or using a word or two to describe the feelings in this area before you begin.

The challenge of iSee energy is to distract the logical mind so the intuitive mind can "speak." Here is an exercise to do just that!

1. Get a deck of cards. Any deck of cards will do—you can use playing cards or cards from a game.

2. Identify an issue you wish to explore and put it in terms of a question using the format, "Is it correct for me to (insert issue)?" For example, the issue might be a leadership challenge with an employee. The question you might ask is "Is it correct for me to fire Suzie?"

3. With that question in mind, begin to flip each card face up. You can neatly stack the cards or simply throw them in a pile.

4. While flipping the cards, speak out loud your responses to the question. Keep talking until you believe you are done with the question. Do you run out of cards before you were done? Simply gather the cards and begin again.

5. When you are done, write down what you have said. Is there anything useful?

The intent is to distract your left-brain through flipping the cards. Your right brain then has the opportunity to "speak." Talking out loud is most effective for this exercise, but you can also do this silently if conditions warrant. If your iSee energy has been taught to doubt itself and shut down, you may need to repeat this exercise frequently to encourage the opening of the iSee energy.

Daniel revisited

Daniel's story is common with high-energy, high-achieving professionals. Their personal goals drive them to success. They are recognized early and often for delivering results for organizational success. The energy, achievement, and recognition result in additional leadership responsibilities. It is highly likely that they will hit a wall, at some time, where their personal success will be impacted. This often occurs when they can no longer achieve results by working harder or individually achieving more. It often happens when they are in the spotlight to inspire others for results.

Because Daniel's early individual results had received recognition and reinforcement, he was blind to the blocked energies that eventually limited his success. As he hits the wall of energy that has been blocked, he has an opportunity to expand and open these energies. Is it an experience you welcome? Most likely not. Is it inevitable? Most likely so.

The key to Daniel's success will be to use his high-energy, high-achieving strength to assist him to open dormant energies. For Daniel, the energies impacted are iConnect and iCare. He will need to address his impatience and frustration with others in order to create the compassion and forgiveness needed to strengthen his leadership. He has always been someone to take on a challenge and succeed. This time, the challenge will be within himself and unlocking his internal keys to success.

The key to unlocking these energies will not be as simple as changing his thoughts. He must allow new ways to open the energy that require intention, attention, and support. Intention comes from clear decisions and declarations about what he wants to be as a leader and how he wants others to experience his leadership. Attention is the commitment to awareness. Awareness is being the observer of oneself. His success has revolved around the awareness of project results. His new awareness needs to become his effectiveness to inspire others. Journaling, coaching, and feedback from others are all examples of tools that can assist his becoming a self-observer to open and expand the iConnect and iCare energies.

We are not designed to become great leaders by ourselves. We need others to support and guide us toward success. While Daniel's success thus far has primarily come from his own hard work, his future success will expand and grow if he is willing to seek support. Mentors, advocates, and champions are needed. This will include direct reports, peers, and advisors, both outside and inside the organization.

Daniel has a choice to make as he hits this blocked wall of energy. The "what to do" is the easy part. The challenge is the choice.

CHAPTER SEVEN

iUnderstand

"I understand my purpose is larger than me."

STEPHANIE'S BOSS, STEVE, is wrapping up the day and heading home to his family. He has just finished a meeting with Stephanie and is thinking how pleased he is with her progress.

"She reminds me of myself!" thought Steve. He would often feel compassion for Stephanie. He has never admitted to Stephanie that he struggles with some of the same issues. The only difference is that he is a few years ahead of Stephanie.

Confidence, clarity of direction, and courage to speak are all energy challenges for Steve. He sits back and thinks about the moment he knew he needed to address these challenges. He was having coffee with Rich, a friend and a mentor. He had been going on and on about how hard he worked and how no one had paid attention. Suddenly Rich stopped him and said, "When are you going to stop whining and do something about it?" Steve laughs as he thinks about how shocked he was to hear this from Rich. It was like a bucket of cold water in his face. Up to that point, he thought he was doing something, but realized that all he was "doing" was complaining!

What happened from that point on was almost miraculous. Rich had suggestions and ideas. He pointed Steve to books, people, and resources. Steve wanted Rich to do it for him, but Rich would not have it. He supported Steve, but encouraged Steve to find his own solutions. Steve chuckles again as he realizes how silly it was to want someone to do it for him. He remembers what a defining moment it was when he made the choice to accept the challenge.

It has been six years since that conversation. Steve has never felt more balanced with who he is, what he wants, and where he will go from here. He certainly has moments where his lack of confidence shows up. Sometimes he hesitates before asking for what he wants, but he recognizes the signals and chooses his direction.

Stephanie has just started the journey he started six years ago. He hopes he is challenging, yet supportive, for Stephanie. Based on today's meeting, things are certainly headed in the right direction!

The Leadership Competencies

Before learning about the iSee and iUnderstand energies, you have been building your sense of who you are and how you will lead others. The five previous energies of **The Leadership Energy Model** have focused on who you trust, how you connect with others, and communication. As you move to iUnderstand, you open a stronger reason to be a leader.

Servant leadership is a term we see in popular leadership publications. Robert Greenleaf, in his book *The Servant as Leader,* states, "The servant-leader is servant first…it begins with the natural feeling that one wants to serve, to serve first. The conscious choice brings one to aspire to lead."

Janet Hagberg's book, *Real Power: Stages of Personal Power in Organizations*, refers to the servant leadership stage as Stage 5, Power By Purpose. Hagberg describes the leadership characteristics in Stage 5 as a leader who strives to be of service to others. The leader provides ideas, support, and encouragement, so as to draw out people at their best. They are non-critical, accepting, and motivate others through empowerment. They have a vision and an understanding that their purpose as a leader goes beyond themselves. There is an opportunity to influence and shift the lives of many.

It is difficult to find behavior competencies for the iUnderstand energy. This leader has a way of "being" a leader. Their attitude and presence brings out the best in others. They have chosen to expand and open all leadership energies and, while they are not "perfect," they maintain a level of self-awareness and self-management to recognize and adjust their energies on a daily basis.

What holds leaders back from opening and using this energy? Often it is the logical left-brain person who needs to have answers. They fear they have too much to lose if they move forward with faith and purpose. The human constraints of fear, achieving results, and the desire for pleasing others limit this energy force.

The Energy Ingredient

The iUnderstand energy is located at the top or crown of your head. Think of this as the door to your thoughts and beliefs. The open iUnderstand energy provides clarity of who you are and expands your purpose in life. This energy partners with the iAchieve energy to bring depth to your career direction. With iAchieve energy, the focus is on defining the plan and having the "fire in one's belly" to make it happen. iUnderstand energy adds the reason "why": why you chose to lead others. Strong iUnderstand energy aligns your higher purpose with your daily actions.

An iUnderstand leader needs to have opened the energies of the other six energies in order to create the foundations for this energy. The fear of iTrust, the people pleasing of iConnect, and the unclear direction of iAchieve are all blocks to opening this energy.

Closed iUnderstand energy occurs when you feel unworthy to have a connection to a larger purpose. Do you wonder, "Who me? Have a larger purpose?" Eastern philosophies would say, "Of course, you!" These philosophies believe you are born with a higher purpose. It is your job to determine that purpose as you progress through life. Your life experiences lead you to understanding this purpose.

Diane was someone who did not believe that she was worthy of a higher purpose. When I met Diane ten years ago, she had advanced to a manager position within her company. She was accomplishing what she needed but her boss wanted her to expand her leadership role.

As Diane and I worked together on her leadership, she described her childhood as one of physical and sexual abuse. She had been placed in one foster home after another. Drugs and alcohol were her solace as a teenager. Despite a tumultuous upbringing, she had taken charge of her life and graduated from college. She was proud to have advanced to her current management position.

When asked what she believed about her purpose as a leader, her response was, "I'm not sure I'm meant to have a purpose. It's been all I can do to survive my life and reach this point in my career." Ten years ago, the concept of a larger purpose for Diane was more than she was ready for. At that time, Diane developed her iAchieve energy through a plan and her iTrust energy through building confidence in herself and others. The iUnderstand energy was not ready to expand and would need to wait.

I have stayed in contact with Diane and we recently met for coffee. She said to me, "Remember when you asked me the question about my larger purpose as a leader?" Of course I did! She went on to say, "I thought that was the most bizarre question. But the question stayed with me. Over time I have realized how many others have the same types of pain from their past. At one point, I had so many peers and direct reports tell me their stories of abuse without my ever mentioning my past. I began to wonder if there was a sign outside my door that read, 'Abuse stories heard here.' I began to realize this was the answer to my purpose question! My purpose is to provide guidance to leaders with wounded souls."

It was gratifying to hear Diane's story. The iUnderstand energy takes time and wisdom to grow and expand. If you believe that we all have a purpose, then, you just need to define yours.

How do you know when you are ready to open this energy? The iUnderstand energy opens when you choose to become non-judgmental about life and events. Judgmental means you evaluate experiences as either good or bad. The western world wants us to label things. But, in iUnderstand energy, we no longer need to label. Instead, you recognize there is a reason that things happen. You need to acknowledge and understand, but not judge. The objective is wisdom and clarity.

Awareness Activities

Engage Your Emotions

In order to open iUnderstand energy, you must first engage the emotions you experience. This is not the typical response, especially to negative emotions. If you feel an emotion like anger, you want to push it away. When you fight the emotions, you increase the emotional reactions. There is a difference between letting the emotions run your life and accepting the emotions you experience.

Let me give you an example. You are hurt by an event in your life. You have been taught that negative emotions are to be ignored. In turn, every time you think of this event, you re-experience the hurt. You label this as a "bad" experience. But, what if you accepted the anger? Yes, you were angry. Yes, the situation was awful. No, you don't need to relive this over and over. You now validate your experience and create acceptance. This goes beyond forgiveness. By choosing acceptance, you decrease the power of the emotional experience, thus allowing you to move forward in your life.

Other Suggestions

Activities to open iUnderstand energy include:

- » Meditation
- » Releasing emotions—picture a bird you release to fly away. You watch the bird. You acknowledge the bird and you allow it to fly away.
- » Prayer
- » Time in nature

Action Learning

The iUnderstand energy that either opens, becomes blocked, or closes is located on the top of your head. Before you begin, focus your awareness on this area.

This action learning exercise contains two steps. Step one is defining your purpose. Step two is bringing your purpose to your daily life.

Step One: Defining Your Purpose

Purpose is not a one-time statement or definition. As we expand and grow, we understand our purpose through our life experiences. Dr. Beatrice Berry, author of *I'm On My Way but Your Foot is on My Head*, has a very simple way of defining purpose. She asks two questions: "Why me?" and "Here now?" She believes that you can answer these two questions any place, any time and your purpose will be self-evident.

Here is another option to Dr. Berry's simple questions.

1. Grab a notebook.

2. You will be documenting your career time line. Create a representation (linear or nonlinear) of all the jobs, paid and volunteer, that you can remember.

3. Once this is complete, go back and reflect on each position. Identify the following:

    » What was your strength?

    » What did you enjoy?

    » What value did you bring?

4. Review the answers to the three questions. What do you notice? Are there patterns to your answers?

5. Write a statement answering the following questions:

    » What has been the purpose of your life so far?

    » How do you share this with others?

    » What do you believe is your purpose as a leader?

This does not need to be long or complicated. As you move forward in life, you will expand this answer based on your life experiences.

Step Two: Bringing Your Purpose To Your Daily Life

The key to leadership is not only knowing your purpose, but also being able to put it into action every day. Here is an exercise to make this happen.

1. Post your purpose statement in a place where you will have easy access.

2. Before you begin each day, review your purpose statement. Then identify three (3) high value leadership activities you can do today that would support your purpose. Here are a few examples and tips to assist you:

    » Call Sue. Send an email to Ken. Listen more than speak at today's meeting.

    » You can see from the examples that these should be specific and measureable. "Be a better leader" is good in concept but not specific and measurable. "Call Sue" is very specific and I can answer, "completed" or "not completed".

    » These do not need to be time intensive. They are small actionable items that support your purpose.

3. Write these three (3) high value items in a place that you will access throughout the day.

4. At the end of your day go back to your list and ask, "Did I complete the three high value leadership activities?" Mark the answer "completed" or "not completed." Do not judge your answers. Just acknowledge them.

5. Repeat steps 1-5 every day.

This is designed to build the habit of purposeful leadership each and every day. This is not cumulative in nature, nor does it require an evaluation or judgment. Each day is a clean slate. With each new day, you determine your focus and measure the outcome.

Stephanie revisited

Stephanie's story is common with dedicated professionals. She cares deeply about her work and works hard to deliver results. As advancement opportunities arise, her quiet dedication is often overlooked.

For Stephanie, the energies needing to open and expand are iTrust, iAchieve, and iSpeak. If she allows others to define her career and life direction for her, she will struggle to advance her leadership. Defining her direction and sharing it with others will be the easiest energies for her to open. Trusting herself and building her confidence will be the greatest struggle. She will need others to support her. Fortunately for Stephanie, her iConnect and iCare energies are open, allowing her to accept the support of others.

Building her confidence through her iTrust energy is an internal process. This energy is formed early in life when experiences were emotional with minimal language or cognitive understanding. Picture Stephanie as a three year old who is afraid of the dark. She experiences fear. The only thing she can attach it to is "dark", even though there may be a myriad of reasons she is fearful. This emotional experience becomes physically embedded as her response to fear.

Now picture the three year old as a thirty-four year old Stephanie. When she encounters a fearful situation, she experiences the same physical fear response as she did when she was three. Her brain begins to interpret the fear as if it is an adult fear. The little girl voice in her head says, "Now is the time they will find out I don't know what I am doing." OR "There is no way I can handle this." She hears these messages as if they are the reality of a thirty-four year old adult, not the voice of a three year old in fear.

What can Stephanie do with this response? First, she needs to recognize fear as the trigger for the "little girl's voice." Then, she needs to do the same thing she would do with a three year old who is afraid of the dark. With a three year old, you would calmly listen, comfort the emotion, and provide a new perspective to calm the fear. What you wouldn't do to a three year old is ignore it or reinforce it. Imagine ignoring a three year old who is afraid of the dark. You would probably hear them scream louder! Or imagine reinforcing it by saying, "You're right! You should be afraid of the dark." It seems ridiculous, right? Yet, how many times do we try to ignore the fear or, worse yet, reinforce it by believing the voice in our head is the voice of a logical, intelligent adult? Stephanie will need to recognize that little girl voice and with the skill of a wise parent, listen, comfort, and provide a new perspective.

Stephanie's strength is her ability to connect with others. She is fortunate to have the support of Steve, her boss. She will also need the support of other mentors, advocates, coaches, and peers. The challenge will be allowing herself to receive support versus always being the one to give support. This will be the choice she will need to make. A small shift in the balance of giving and receiving will create a huge shift in Stephanie trusting herself, being assertive in asking for what she needs, and advancing her leadership success.

PART FOUR

Putting It All Together

You have now experienced **The Leadership Energy Model** through stories, leadership competencies, understanding the energy ingredient and action learning activities. What's next?

CHAPTER EIGHT

Where To From Here?

YOU ARE A work in progress. **The Leadership Energy Model** recognizes you will never be done. You are impacted daily as you navigate the journey of life.

Awareness is key. How is your energy today? Where might you have blocks? It is my hope that this book gives you short-term tactics along with long-term strategies to recognize and impact your healthy flow of energy. The healthier your energy, the more effective and successful leader you will be.

What's next? It is up to you to define yourself as a leader. Ask yourself the following questions:

- » What do I hope to be as a leader?
- » How do I want others to experience my leadership?
- » What will I experience as an effective leader?
- » Why is this important to me?

To assist you in answering these questions, I surveyed twenty-eight individuals and asked them to describe an effective leader. These are individuals who currently work in a variety of organizations, both large and small. They were asked to think of someone they see as an effective leader. Six themes emerged from the survey. Here are the six themes along with comments from the survey participants. You can find all of the survey responses in the appendix.

» *They have a presence.*

> » *The person I am thinking of is a good communicator—know when to tell, when to teach, when to coach, when to listen and when to be quiet. BUD*

> » *In a confident, almost charismatic and very friendly voice, my leader looks me in the eye and delivers compelling statements which tell me he genuinely cares about the business, the customer, and the team (me) in a balanced manner. He provides enough information to demonstrate thoughtful consideration, provides direction, asks what help I need, and makes time for me when I ask for 15 minutes to chat during which I always have his complete, undivided attention. GB*

» *They intentionally share themselves with others.*

> » *He was very personable and garnered trust quickly. He backed that up with knowledge. He surrounded himself with people that could get the job done and he put a lot of trust in us to make that happen but he was always there to help out if needed. RT*

> » *Confidence—and willingness to listen to ideas different from their own. If I have a meeting time with them, they are fully engaged and on time. My time with them is as important to them as it is to me. Ability to reach all levels of the organization with the consistent message of the vision and*

values and how individuals make a difference; an effective communicator to all levels of the organization. RL

» **They provide hope.**

> » *She takes pains to recognize and appreciate each person's contributions to the project. She has a vision for a result and is able to articulate it and get others to help the vision become a reality. She is inclusive. JM*

> » *This person has a purpose that is much larger than he is, and a personality and skills sets that are balanced. He has used his skills and his personality traits to put his purpose into action. HS*

» **I feel valued.**

> » *He clears the rocks and boulders blocking my path, helps me logic through difficult issues and situations when I ask for guidance/sounding board, allows me to stumble but not to fail miserably. He coaches and encourages, praises in public, scolds in private, takes the blame, shares the credit for success. He never micromanages. He will encourage me, providing opportunities to stretch my skills and experience to higher levels of performance. He is as interested in my success and effectiveness as in his own. GB*

> » *I experience a knowledge they support me, empower me, trust me to do the right thing in the right way without micromanaging me. The experience creates an openness, flexibility and agility—the comfort that you are working together on a team going in the same way. RL*

» **I feel heard.**

> » *They aren't attached to only their way to do what needs to be done and they get out of my way as I work thru it and*

trust me to deliver and let them know when they need to help me. PS

» *I feel 'heard' on many levels....I experience congruency between what is said and what is done.....I see the example of servant leadership being lived out. KMN*

» **I feel support to grow.**

    » *People follow them not because of position but because they believe in them. Feel good about yourself and empowered to take something to the next level. Supported in decision making. Allowed to take risks. MF*

    » *The feeling that they are on top of the issues facing the business, the feeling that my input and actions are important to their decision making and to the success of the business. The feeling of being connected to that person. TE*

Let me end this book by leaving you with a story.

The Magic Key to Happiness and Success

There is an ancient legend about a time in the history of humanity when society so abused wisdom that sidemen decided to take the secret of happiness and success away from man and hide it where mankind would never find it again. The big question was where to hide it? A council was called by the chief of the Wisemen to discuss this question. The lesser of the Wisemen said, "We will bury the secret of happiness and success into the dark depths of the earth."

The chief Wiseman responded, "No, that will never do, for mankind will dig deep down in the earth and find it."

Then they said, "Well, we will sink the secret of happiness and success into the dark depths of the deepest ocean."

But again, the chief Wiseman replied, "No, not there, for humankind will surely learn to dive into the dark depths of the ocean and will find it."

Then, one of the Wisemen said, "We will take it to the top of the highest mountain and hide it there."

But again the Wiseman said, "No, for humankind will eventually climb even the highest mountain and find it, and again take it up for themselves."

Then, the chief Wiseman said, "Here is what we will do with the secret of happiness and success, we will hide it deep inside every individual, for they will never think to look for it there."

To this day according to legend, people have been running back and forth across the earth—digging, diving, and climbing, in search of something that they already possess within themselves.

As a leader, you have the opportunity to stop the running back and forth, the digging, diving, and climbing in search of something that already lies within you. It's time to go forth and unlock the secrets to your leadership success!

Appendix
Leadership Survey

I ASKED TWENTY-EIGHT people to answer two questions related to their experience of an effective leader. They were asked to think of a real person and answer two questions. Below are the two questions and the individual responses.

1. **Think of someone you know that you view as an effective leader. This needs to be a real person. What do they _do_ that creates the impression they are an effective leader?**

    » _She takes pains to recognize and appreciate each person's contributions to the project. She has a vision for a result and is able to articulate it and get others to help the vision become a reality. She is inclusive. JM, Professor_

    » _They listen calmly...really listen not just pause; ask smart insightful questions and then decide...even if the final decision is different from her original thought. They make things happen that were good for others. LG, Author_

» *When I produce good results as an affect of their positive leadership then I believe they were a good mentor to me. EB*

» *They demonstrate compassion and confidence. GB, Architect*

» *She waited and watched while the dominant horse who "did" things that gave the impression of being leader, such as herd horses to one end of the arena, separate the mares from the geldings, etc., made lots of stir. She conserved energy while staying present. LB, Coach*

» *The person I thinking of is a good communicator—know when to tell, when to teach, when to coach, when to listen and when to be quiet. BUD, Health Insurance*

» *Asks the difficult question. Addresses conflict directly and (mostly) non defensively. Makes decisions in the face of uncertainty without drama. Direct eye contact. Emotionally appropriate. JE, Coach*

» *He was very personable and garnered trust quickly. He backed that up with knowledge. He surrounded himself with people that could get the job done and he put a lot of trust in us to make that happen but he was always there to help out if needed. RT, Architect*

» *This person has a purpose that is much larger than he is and a personality and skills sets that are balanced. He has used his skills and his personality traits to put his purpose into action. HS, Manager*

» *They dress for success and create a commanding presence when they walk into the room. RB, Lawyer/CPA*

» *In a confident, almost charismatic and very friendly voice my leader looks me in the eye and delivers compelling statements which tell me he genuinely cares about the business, the customer, and the team (me) in a balanced manner. He provides enough information to demonstrate thoughtful consideration, provides direction, asks what help I need, and makes time for me when I ask for 15 minutes to chat during which I always have his complete, undivided attention. GB*

» *Confidence—and willingness to listen to ideas different from their own. If I have a meeting time with them, they are fully engaged and on time. My time with them is as important to them as it is to me. Ability to reach all levels of the organization with the consistent message of the vision and values and how individuals make a difference; an effective communicator to all levels of the organization. RL, Human Resources*

» *The consistent desire to reach a common goal that everyone can buy into consistent with the values and vision of the organization. SS, Executive Director*

» *A person that I know that is an effective leader is very professional, consistent and lives an example of high integrity and is brutally honest. He does his homework and often knows the answer to questions before he asks them. He has a large presence and exudes confidence. He has his finger on the pulse of all parts of the organization and is rarely surprised by anything operational. When faced with issues, he breaks them down into pieces to analyze and doesn't seem to get emotional about them. I have also observed that he is a planner--he works from a "to do" list that is frequently reprioritized. TR*

» *She is genuinely interested in making sure we understand the topic by asking for responses, repeatedly. And says, "come on people, wake up," when we are shy to respond. Makes us accountable. BH*

» *They stay in contact with what is going on and the people involved. As a result, they know the situation and make sound decisions, which are actually implemented on a timely basis. AS, Manager*

» *They listen and remember. They value the team, they adjust based on what's needed now to get us to where we want to go. They are honest and authentic. They share their struggles and challenges and bring you into their world. PS, Director*

» *Authentic...does and behaves as they say they will. Acts with confidence and optimism. Good energy. MF, Non-profit*

» *Completely committed to well-articulated vision, e.g. they always keep the team focused on what each and everyone of them and their work makes possible and why that is important. JA, Coach*

» *It appears that they are usually available to answer, respond to and/*

or meet with potential new clients fairly quickly. Also available to their team when needed. Not overscheduled. RA, Operations

» *This person shows genuine interest in me personally and my capability to be a contribution in the world. This personal displays integrity and authenticity......leads with a servant heart......and relies on others' strengths and perspectives for greater results. KMN, Coach*

» *He asks the right questions, listens to the answer and guides the group to a course of action. They ensure the customer is satisfied, addresses problems head on, and uses them as a learning opportunity. TE, Human resources*

» *The make decisions rather than just talk about issues without taking action. CO, Engineer*

» *My brother is a born leader. He takes direction and gets things done fast and clearly. SB, Writer*

» *Mentoring. Not just professing to being a mentor, but actually acting like a mentor by having candid conversations about their team members' strengths and opportunities for improvement, and then providing chances for those team members to shine—without taking credit for having helped them get there. MK, Communications Specialist*

2. **What do *you experience* that makes you believe they are an effective leader?**

» *I experience a sense of anticipation--eagerness to make a contribution that will serve the project because I know my efforts will be appreciated. I get the feeling that the project is under control (not controlled but on track to a destination). JM, Professor*

» *What I experienced is the effect her confidence has on the teams' ability to act well as one unit. I experienced seeing the example of how a truly selfless act can have benefits far beyond anything we can imagine. LG, Author*

» *If I mess up, they allow me to experience the pain or hardship for the error, but they also forgive me for my wrong doing and give me advice on how to make things better based on their own experiences with achievement. EB*

» *EXCITEMENT AND A DESIRE TO ACT LIKE THEM GB, Architect*

» *When the dominant horse came over and tried to herd her, all she did was twitch an ear and he backed off. No fuss or fluster. Her grounded energy and clear communication completely engaged him, and also took his attention away from stirring up the other horses, freeing them up to interact more peacefully and cooperatively. LB, Coach*

» *I experience a trust in the person—both that they are trustworthy and future-focused! BUD, Health insurance*

» *A sense of confidence. Emotional control. Calm. JE, Coach*

» *I felt that he cared about me and my success because I directly affected the success of the office by my work. I felt I had to be successful to not let him down as he placed a lot of trust in me. Even though he was an authority figure (which I normally have apprehension about), he made me feel comfortable and needed. RT, Architect*

» *He is passionate toward others, he holds great values and interpersonal skills, he is visionary, and he is very knowledgeable, he is a great planner and organizer, and above all he is an outstanding communicator (both orally and in writing). I think his communication skills is the main cause I consider this person an effective leader, because without his ability to communicate effectively his other characteristics will never be evident. HS, Manager*

» *They solve problems. They find solutions. . RH, Lawyer/CPA*

» *He clears the rocks and boulders blocking my path, helps me logic through difficult issues and situations when I ask for guidance/ sounding board, allows me to stumble but not to fail miserably. He coaches and encourages, praises in public, scolds in private, takes the blame, shares the credit for success. He never micromanages. He will encourage me, providing opportunities to stretch my skills and experience to higher levels of performance. He is as interested in my success and effectiveness as in his own. GB*

» *I experience a knowledge they support me, empower me, trust me to do the right thing in the right way without micromanaging me. The experience creates an openness, flexibility and agility—the comfort that you are working together on a team going in the same way. RL, Human resources*

» *This individual is able to create consensus on a regular basis involving issues that have strong opposing viewpoints. This is achieved through pragmatism, objectivity and gentle persuasion. SS, Executive Director*

» *Sometimes I personally experience nervousness or maybe some insecurity, but usually, he makes me want to perform at an "A" level and make sure that I have done my homework. I can see that co-workers respect him and also want to make sure they have their "A" game on--no one wants to be caught off guard with something that he knows and they didn't but should have known. TR*

» *The immediate, and frequent, interactive feedback is a positive step towards the goal or objective. I experience small levels of accomplishment, similar to climbing steps. Makes me present in the moment, often. BH*

» *I converse with this person (using "converse" on purpose here—not speaking to, but actually having a conversation is key), witness that they converse with others, and see them implement decisions that are not always easy. AS, Manager*

» *They aren't attached to only their way to do what needs to be done and they get out of my way as I work thru it and trust me to deliver and let them know when they need to help me. PS, Director*

» *People follow them not because of position but because they believe in them. Feel good about yourself and empowered to take something to the next level. Supported in decision making. Allowed to take risks. MF, Non-profit*

» *A calm determination that invites others to respect each other's needs (psychologically and physiologically!) while they're all gettin er done. JA, Coach*

» *I feel 'heard' on many levels....I experience congruency between what is said and what is done.....I see the example of servant leadership being lived out. KMN, Coach*

» *The feeling that they are on top of the issues facing the business, the feeling that my input and actions are important to their decision making and to the success of the business. The feeling of being connected to that person. TE, Human Resources*

» *A sense of progress. CO, Engineer*

» *He is passionate about helping people with the knowledge he has learned. SB, Writer*

» *A feeling of being supported, even when mistakes are made, while simultaneously feeling independent / being allowed to have autonomous decision-making. A bit dichotomous, yes, but possible. MK, Communications Specialist*

Acknowledgements

There are many who have contributed to this book.

Let me start by recognizing two important experts. First is my writing coach, Joe Moses. With his help I found confidence and focus. His skillful questioning and suggestions led me to clarity of what and how this book would come together.

The second important expert is Wendy Hack (yes, that is her real name). Her editing allowed me to be clear in the message.

Last, but not least, is a wonderful group of people I called my Advisory Board. They volunteered to read and provide feedback as I wrote this book. Their honest feedback was greatly appreciated and incorporated.

- » Ann Baumer Schulte, Medtronic
- » Barbara Brodsho
- » Chad O'Donnell, HGA Architects and Engineers
- » Cynthia A. Scott
- » Dr. Angela Bremer

- » Gabrielle A. Bullock, AIA, NOMA, LEED AP BD+C, Perkins+Will
- » Gail P. Baumer, West Bend Mutual Insurance
- » Hojat Shahghasemi, Medtronic
- » Jim Earley, Trailblazer Coaching
- » Jonathan J. Abramson, avenue2possibilities LLC
- » Julie Hagstrom
- » Laura Gilbert, Ph.D., Back to School for Grownups
- » Louise Griffith, MA, LP, One Shining Light
- » Lynn Baskefield, Wisdom Horse Coaching
- » Marcia Fink, Greater Twin Cities United Way
- » Margie Komp, MBC, HID Global
- » Pam Stegman
- » Rachel Wetzsteon, PhD
- » Renee C. Aloisio, LGC+D, LLP
- » Richard R. Tannahill, AIA
- » Roben D. Hunter, JD, CPA, CVA, MAFF, Boeckermann Grafstrom & Mayer, LLC
- » Steven E. Sacks, CPA, ABC, Moore Stephens North America, Inc.
- » Suzanne Bundt
- » Teresa A. Ranallo, CPA
- » Thomas Emig
- » Wendy Brennan, http://Plan4Prosperity.com/

Resource list

The following resources were used to support the content of this book.

Bio-energy

King, Deborah. *Truth Heals.* HayHouse, 2010.

Tuttle, Carol. *Chakra Healing.* Mind Valley Academy, 2002.

Tuttle, Carol. *Chakra 7.* Mind Valley Academy, 2012.

Coaching

Baskfield, Lynn. *Wisdom Horse Coaching.*

Tryhus, Christy. *Live Life Beyond the Laundry: Seven Strategies to shift life from chaos to calm.* Christy Tryhus, 2012.

Leadership

Covey, Steven. *7 Habits of Highly Effective People.* FreePress, 2004.

Greenleaf, Robert K. *The Servant as Leader.* Greenleaf Center for Servant Leadership, 2008.

Hagberg, Janet. *Real Power: Stages of Personal Power in Organizations.* Sheffield Publishing Co., 2003.

Hughes, Robert, Ginnett, Robert, Curphy, Gordon. *Leadership: Enhancing the Lessons of Experience.* McGraw-Hill/Irvin, 2011.

Rock, David. *Your Brain at Work.* Harper Business, 2009.

Purpose

Berry, Beatrice. *I'm On My Way but Your Foot is on My Head.* Scribner, 1997.

McDonald, Bob and Hutcheson, Don. *Don't Waste Your Talent.* The Highlands Company, 2010.

Warren, Rich. *The Purpose Driven Life: What on Earth Am I Here For?* Zondervan Publishers, 2012.

Visit www.TheLeadershipEnergy.com

You will find additional tools and resources to
support your Leadership Energy Journey!

THE LEADERSHIP ENERGY MODEL

CPSIA information can be obtained at www.ICGtesting.com
Printed in the USA
BVOW05s0256020414

349428BV00003B/7/P